northumbrian coastline

Berwick-upon-Tweed to North Shields

Ian Smith

SANDHILL PRESS

Acknowledgments

My thanks go to all who have encouraged me to put pen to paper, and to all those who have loaned me photographs, shared their knowledge and offered accommodation in Northumberland.

To all of my family

The section maps are to a scale of 1:45000 and are based upon the Landranger Map of the Ordnance Survey with the permission of Her Majesty's Stationery Office. Crown Copyright Reserved.

First published in Great Britain by Sandhill Press Ltd., Castleside, 40 Narrowgate, Alnwick, Northumberland, NE66 1JQ, 1988

© Ian Smith 1988

ISBN 0 946098 10 7

Printed by Martin's of Berwick, bound by Hunter & Foulis in Great Britain.

Contents

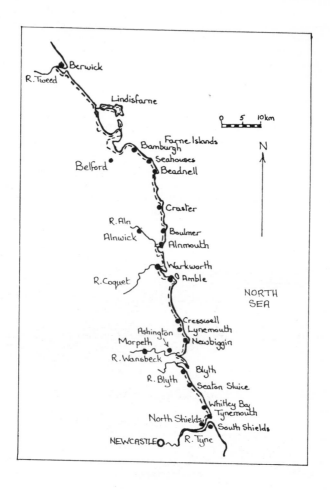

INTRODUCTION

Northumberland keeps its coast secret from the casual passer-by. From the A1 there are tantalising glimpses of the sea and the Farne Islands. From the train there are sudden views of Alnmouth: red roofs and white sands. There are dramatic panoramas across Fenham Flats to Holy Island, and clifftop scenes near Berwick. Even from the coastal roads the shore itself stays hidden behind the dunes once you are north of the Wansbeck.

But if you are not in a hurry, if you are prepared to leave your car or bus or train and walk a little, there is much to discover. This guide is intended to encourage you to explore.

Beyond those dunes stretch vast beaches of glorious sand: Druridge Bay is seven miles of golden strand; Blyth, Warkworth, Alnmouth and Embleton have long golden sands too, whilst Bamburgh Beach has miles of silky white sand.

On Cresswell Beach

There is enough beach for everyone here. Even on hot days, with several hundred people along Druridge Bay you may be a quarter-mile or so from the next person. Yet even in winter they are seldom totally deserted.

5

Between the beaches are short sections of cliff, where the harder rocks resist the erosion of the elements. Here the bones of the land lie revealed. Geologists, and indeed anyone with any appreciation of rocks or patterns will enjoy these stretches. The various layers of rock lie open to inspection, forming wicked reefs across or along the shore, or great pavements revealed by the retreating tide. There are swirls of colour and texture in the cliffs as one rock succeeds another.

Small but fascinating bays huddle between headlands of resistant rock, and rock-pools offer a fascinating habitat to observe.

Rock strata and pools, by Rumbling Kern Howick

Hard rock is the base for the coast's best-known landmarks too: the great castles of Bamburgh, Dunstanburgh and Lindisfarne sit on outcrops of the Whin Sill. These remind us of the county's border status (as do the castles at Berwick, Warkworth and Tynemouth, plus the many inland castles).

Warkworth Castle

But the history of this region is expressed not just by reminders of war. The Celtic tradition of Christianity, nurtured on Holy Island, expanded from here, leaving much more than a few buildings and a local name for eider ducks!

Industry too has made its mark. It is still very obvious in the South-Eastern corner of the County, where there is still a continuing cycle of new industry replacing old. Lynemouth is very obviously industrial, with its coal-processing plant, power station and aluminium smelter. Seaton Sluice, on the other hand, seems remote from industrial influence. Yet this was the very heart of Northumberland's industry for centuries, until quite recently. Even Holy Island had its limestone, with quarries, tramways, kilns and export quay, at one time. Fascinating reminders of this industrial heritage lie scattered along the coast for the observant to find.

Fishing is one industry that has declined markedly. Boats still ply from the many little harbours and havens, but relatively few now. The great herring fleets have disappeared, leaving the distinctive deep-prowed cobles for the local specialised catches, and a handful of trawlers operating from the larger ports.

Tractor and trailer wait to land a coble, at Newbiggin

The coastal villages have their own character too. Most are exposed to the blasts from the North Sea. They sit firmly anchored on outcrops of rock, with inter-tidal rocks breaking the fury of the sea. But they have a rugged, austere look. Some, such as Bamburgh and Warkworth, are sheltered from the sea and have a softer, more rural appearance.

Near the Tyne the villages have run together to form a continuous but variegated townscape: Cullercoats is still distinct from its neighbours — Whitley Bay and Tynemouth.

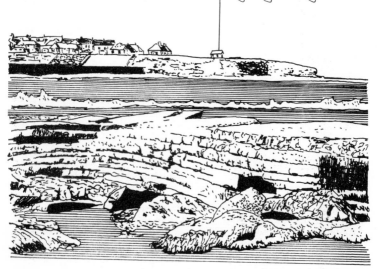

Cullercoats

The Guide

This includes a continuous strip map of the coast to a scale of 1:45000, from Berwick to North Shields, with notes and comments to assist those who want to walk along this coast and discover its secrets and joys.

It is not intended as a single long-distance walk. Much more of the coastal character can be appreciated by a series of short walks, taking time to stop, look and explore. Picking your way along the rock pools is more rewarding than eating up the miles. The buses serving the coast allow a wide range of one-way walks if carefully planned.

8

RIGHTS OF WAY, TIDES and COASTAL WALKING

The route indicated on the sketch maps is NOT evidence of a right of way. The shore between the tide-lines is mainly the property of the Crown, and there is seldom any objection to its use as a thoroughfare on foot. BUT it is not always passable or safe. There are many sections of the coastal walk where the best route is along the beach, so choose the time of your trips carefully to match the tide. (Tide times are published in the local newspapers). Avoid being trapped against cliffs or private property by the incoming tide. In particular take care on the flats of Goswick, Fenham and Budle Bay: the tide rushes in very quickly over the flat sands.

Major river crossings are made by bridge or ferry. But several of the smaller streams that flow into the sea can offer awkward or dangerous crossings. Be prepared to make a diversion if the conditions are against a safe passage.

Berwick Old Bridge

Notes on route-finding are brief. Except on the diversions inland the sea itself is a fairly reliable guide to the coastline and there is little scope for mistakes.

Rights of way ARE indicated on Ordnance Survey Maps. Useful sheets are:

1:50 000	Sheet 75,	Berwick upon Tweed
	Sheet 81,	Alnwick and Morpeth
	Sheet 88,	Tyneside.

These sheets also offer much other information about the areas inland from the coast, and about the relief of the coastal strip itself, and can add much to your understanding and appreciation of what you see.

9

When using field paths or lanes, respect the countryside:
— Shut gates.
— Keep dogs under control. Where there is livestock keep them on a lead.
— Stay on the path. Do not wander on the crops. Remember that grass is an expensive and important crop!
— Guard against fire.
— Leave farm machinery, boats, crops and livestock alone.
— Take your litter home. Even a can ring-pull or a plastic bag can maim or kill.
— Respect wildlife, animals, sea-creatures, plants and trees. There is much to see, especially bird-life and flowers. Look, but do not interfere.

Below the bathing house, Howick

SENSIBLE WEAR

The weather along the coast can change very rapidly. A snow squall can reach you from the horizon quicker than you can walk a mile back to shelter. A hot summer's day can become distinctly chilly if the wind gets up from the sea. The descent of the North Sea roak, as cool sea air creeps in under still, warm land air to produce a belt of fog, brings both cold and loss of visibility to too many summer days.
So be prepared. In summer pack your cagoule and pullover as well as your sun-tan cream and swim-wear!
In winter, when the sea breeze can be bitterly cold, thermal wear, anoraks, woollen hats and mittens can be essential.

Sensible foot-wear needs thought too. Heavy boots are not the best wear for soft sandy beaches. Mud-flats may require wellingtons. Rocks and clifftops require more than town shoes or sandals. Select your footwear to match the route ahead.

Also remember to carry a watch : tides and buses wait for no man!
Binoculars are very useful too : there are large numbers of birds to see, and passing shipping.

ACCOMMODATION

There are villages every few miles along the coast, with inns, hotels and bed-and-breakfast accommodation. In summer this can be heavily booked, so it is wise to book ahead. The information centres may be able to help with addresses and telephone numbers.

Cottages and caravans can be hired at some locations. Campsites are scarce. Waren Mill and Beadnell are conveniently situated. The Wansbeck Riverside Park at Ashington is inland but pleasant.

Caravanners fare somewhat better. In addition to the Ashington park there are sites at East Ord (near Berwick), Haggerston Castle, Waren Mill, Seahouses, Beadnell, Sandy Bay (Newbiggin) and near Whitley Bay.

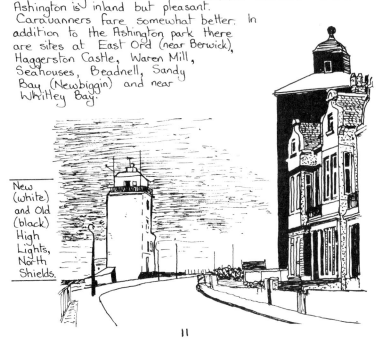

New (white) and Old (black) High Lights, North Shields.

Roads and Buses.

The coast is seldom far from a road, and a network of buses parallels it closely.

The Newcastle to Berwick service is very useful, linking many parts of the coast either directly or via changes at Belford, Alnwick or Morpeth.

There are buses to Holy Island some days.

A good service links Belford with Alnwick via Bamburgh, Seahouses, Beadnell, and Craster.

Other services link Alnwick through Alnmouth, Warkworth, Amble and Widdrington, to Morpeth or Ashington.

Cresswell, Lynemouth and Newbiggin have services to Ashington and/or Newcastle.

There is a sparse service to Cambois and North Blyth.

From Blyth southwards there is a frequent service of buses on the coast road through Seaton Sluice, Whitley Bay and Tynemouth.

Bus routes and times are subject to frequent change. Check with the operator for the current situation.

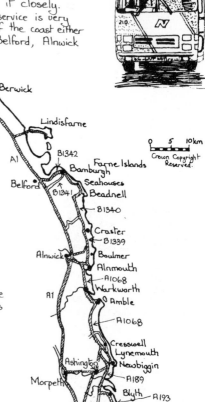

12

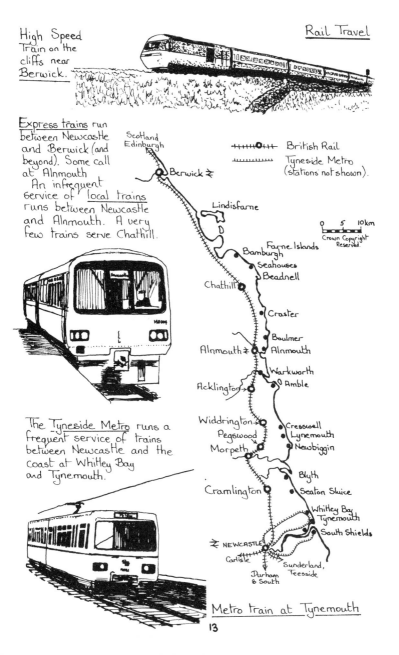

High Speed Train on the cliffs near Berwick.

Express trains run between Newcastle and Berwick (and beyond). Some call at Alnmouth

An infrequent service of local trains runs between Newcastle and Alnmouth. A very few trains serve Chathill.

The Tyneside Metro runs a frequent service of trains between Newcastle and the coast at Whitley Bay and Tynemouth.

Scotland Edinburgh

Berwick

Lindisfarne

+++++O+++ British Rail

Tyneside Metro (stations not shown).

0   5   10km
Crown Copyright
Reserved.

Farne Islands
Bamburgh
Seahouses
Beadnell

Chathill

Craster

Boulmer
Alnmouth   Alnmouth

Warkworth
Amble

Acklington

Widdrington   Cresswell
Pegswood   Lynemouth
Morpeth   Newbiggin

Blyth
Seaton Sluice

Cramlington

Whitley Bay
Tynemouth
South Shields

NEWCASTLE
Carlisle   Sunderland,
Teesside
Durham
& South

Metro train at Tynemouth

13

Berwick upon Tweed.

is a very Scottish town, for all that it is now in England. It is an English town but a Scottish royal burgh. It is in Northumberland, but just to the north is the Scottish District of Berwickshire. Its football team plays in the Scottish League, its banks are mainly Scottish, yet its police, schools and local buses are English (or perhaps more properly North-umbrian). Geographically it ought to be in Scotland, for it lies on the north bank of the Tweed. It is armies and politics that have diverted the border a few miles to the north. In the past it has changed hands between the kingdoms (up to 1482 thirteen times) and has from time to time been accorded a status alongside the larger divisions of the U.K. Thus Berwick declared war in the Crimean conflict (although it did not figure in the peace treaty – is it still at war with Russia?)

As a border town it has its own unique flavour, and a good preamble to an exploration of the Northumberland coast is to walk the circuit of the Elizabethan ramparts.

The Royal
Border Bridge.

* A good starting point is the railway station, at the north-west corner of the town. From the west side of the station bridge a path goes down through pleasant gardens past the Castle ruins:
• Berwick Castle dates back to Edward I, and occupies a mound at the top of the town, overlooking the town and the river. It was supplanted by the Elizabethan fortifications, and suffered greatly when the railway was built through it! A long curtain wall stretches down to a gun-position (ruined) on the riverbank.

* As you descend through the gardens, the path seems to be going to take you upriver. But below the hedge at the bottom a path runs back towards the town. It passes through short tunnels under the ruined battery, and becomes a pleasant walk under the trees beside the river. Pass under the great railway viaduct (126' (40 metres) high – built in 1847), and on below the cliffs and walls that protect the town.

14

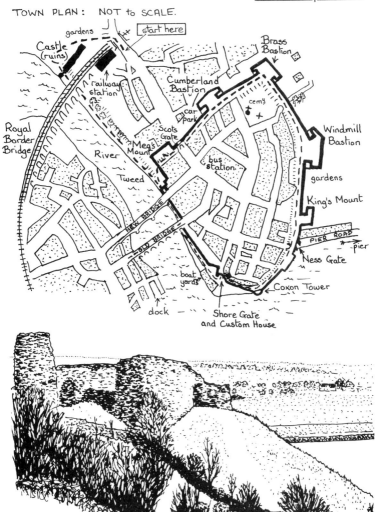

TOWN PLAN: NOT to SCALE.

gardens

Castle (ruins)

start here

Brass Bastion

Cumberland Bastion

railway station

car park

cemy

Scots Gate

Meg's Mount

bus station

Windmill Bastion

gardens

King's Mount

Royal Border Bridge

River

Tweed

NEW BRIDGE

OLD BRIDGE

PIER ROAD

pier

Ness Gate

boat yards

dock

Coxon Tower

Shore Gate and Custom House

Berwick Castle ruins, above the River Tweed.

15

Berwick

* Continue along the riverside path towards the road bridges. On your left, above the trees, the natural walls and banks rise up to the fortifications of Meg's Mount. On the river you will probably see swans in large numbers. Go on past the rowing club boathouse, and under the first road-bridge.

● The New Bridge (or Royal Tweed Bridge officially) is a solid twentieth century essay in concrete. It was opened in 1928 to relieve the older bridge of the heavy traffic of the A1.

● More interesting is the Old Bridge – fifteen arches striding across the river. It dates back to 1611-24, and is reputed to have been built following caustic comments by James I (James VI of Scotland). He had to cross the river on the previous rickety wooden bridge, on his way south to take up the throne of England. Certainly a new, solid bridge over the Tweed was a good symbol of the new United Kingdom.

* Cross the road at the north end of the Old Bridge, and follow the footpath along the house fronts on top of Quay Walls. This gives a good view down over the quays and boatyards. If you wish to descend, steps lead down beside the arch at the Shoregate.

The New Bridge, from Meg's Mount.

* Keep on the walls beyond Shore gate, passing the Custom House to reach the Main Guard. Here a long line of gun platforms show where the battery to command the river was sited.

Coxon's Tower

Coxon's Tower follows, then Fisher's Fort, both with fine views to the rivermouth. The Ness, on the north bank, terminates with a pier and lighthouse, whilst the headland on the south shore is dominated by the chimney at Spittal.

The path turns north, and climbs up over Ness Gate and up onto King's Mount.

Russian cannon on Fisher's Fort - captured at Sebastopol. Its pair is on the promenade at Dartmouth in Devon. Note the wheels.

Berwick

• <u>The Elizabethan ramparts</u> are a symbol of the age of artillery.
Gone are the thin curtain walls of stone, hallmark of the
mediœval castle. They are replaced by thick earth-works,
served by a network of tunnels. A series of bastions
protects the wall, and each other. Cannon hidden in the
flankers can hail withering fire on any foolish enough to
attack the walls. Careful geometry ensures that every wall
is thus protected. Guided tours are sometimes available.

Berwick

* Follow the ramparts round the northern side of the town. In succession you will pass King's Mount, Windmill, Brass & Cumberland Bastions. (At none of them is the named object visible!). The gardens, greens, views and trees make it a very attractive walk.

The wall brings you to Scots Gate, where you cross above the old Great North Road, to Meg's Mount (named after Queen Margaret) This is a superb vantage point for views over the bridges and the town.

You can descend into the town by Scots Gate, if you wish to visit the shops (or other places of interest, such as the Town Hall (left)). Alternatively, a footpath will lead you down to the New Bridge.

The way south is over the Old Bridge (for tradition's sake) or the New (for views).

Town Hall (1754)

Scots Gate & Meg's Mount

19

Berwick to Spittal

You have a choice of bridges leaving Berwick. The older, lower bridge is perhaps more aesthetically pleasing to the pedestrian — and more romantic — but the New Bridge does offer better views: upstream to the Royal Border Bridge and downstream over the Berwick Bridge towards the river-mouth.

If you do choose the higher bridge, bear left at its south end past a little garden, and back down the slope to meet the road from the lower bridge.

Follow the road through Tweedmouth, past the dock with its attendant warehouses. Continuing, you can walk along a grassy promenade beside the river. This is where the railway sidings, and an incline up to the main line, used to be. You can see the level of the latter by the track maintenance depot up the hill. An archway on the right shows where the branch crossed a road on one leg of its zigzag descent. (The bridge over your road has been demolished).

The river is home to very many swans. You may also see cormorants perching on the pilings, and other sea-birds.

Go on past the lifeboat station, and pick a way out past the factory to Sandstell Point, at the mouth of the Tweed. A footpath goes on, over grass, past the factory fence towards Spittal.

The Life-boat House at Tweedmouth.

20

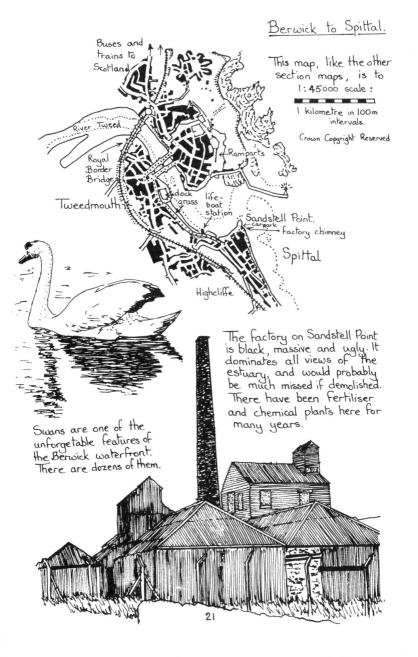

Berwick to Spittal.

This map, like the other section maps, is to 1:45000 scale:

1 kilometre in 100m intervals.

Buses and trains to Scotland

River Tweed

Royal Border Bridge

Tweedmouth

dock grass

life-boat station

Ramparts

Sandstell Point.
carpark
factory chimney

Spittal

Highcliffe

Swans are one of the unforgetable features of the Berwick waterfront. There are dozens of them.

The factory on Sandstell Point is black, massive and ugly. It dominates all views of the estuary, and would probably be much missed if demolished. There have been fertiliser and chemical plants here for many years.

Sandstell Point to Scremerston Sea House

* The grassy path past the factory takes you to <u>Spittal Promenade</u>. A sandy beach is separated from a terrace of houses by a wall and a road. Walk along past the 'Pavilion' — a little entertainment centre — and the rest of the little resort. Near the end of the promenade a path slants upwards (above and behind a block of toilets). It joins a track that continues up onto the clifftops. You may see a train here: the main line runs parallel to your path for a short way.

The slope of the cliffs is determined by the dip-slope of the Scremerston Series of rocks. The wide variety of rocks is very obvious, and there are signs of mining in past times : ruins and pony tracks. Go on past Sea House, on the track.

Cliffs towards Sea House

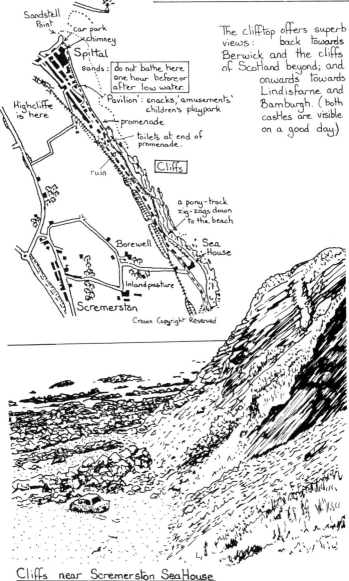

Sandstell Point to Scremerston Seahouse

Sandstell Point

car park

chimney

Spittal

sands:

do not bathe here
one hour before or
after low water.

'Pavilion': snacks, 'amusements'
children's playpark

Highcliffe
is here

promenade

toilets at end of
promenade.

ruin

Cliffs

a pony-track
zig-zags down
to the beach

Borewell

Sea
House

Inland pasture

Scremerston

Crown Copyright Reserved

The clifftop offers superb
views: back towards
Berwick and the cliffs
of Scotland beyond; and
onwards towards
Lindisfarne and
Bamburgh. (both
castles are visible
on a good day.)

Cliffs near Scremerston SeaHouse

23

Cocklawburn Beach.

* Follow the lane down from Sea House to Cocklawburn Beach. Note how the rock strata are in a different direction ahead: instead of running parallel to the shoreline and forming the dip-slope of the cliffs, now they stick out from the shore as a series of fangs. If the tide permits, the shore is the best route as it takes you over one set of rock and then another. Here are different colours, shapes, textures. There are slabs of limestone pavement; hard, pale-grey and jointed into blocks. There are tilted beds of limestone lumps sitting on top of sandstone. There are jagged areas of different-coloured sandstones — and golden sand between.

If the tide is high, you may have to follow the lane to its end, and the rough trackway over the dunes.

Beyond the prominent ruinous limekiln the beach starts to settle down to uniformity: golden sands backed by dunes. This scenery is much in evidence between here and Cresswell. Ahead of you the castles of Lindisfarne and Bamburgh may be visible if the weather is kind.

Cheswick Black Rocks, and the dunes.

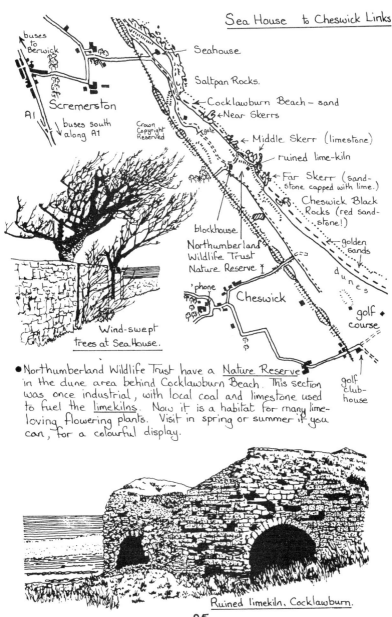

buses to Berwick

Scremerston

A1

↓ buses south along A1

Crown Copyright Reserved

Seahouse

Saltpan Rocks.

Cocklawburn Beach – sand

Near Skerrs

gate

Middle Skerr (limestone)

ruined lime-kiln

Far Skerr (sand-stone capped with lime.)

Cheswick Black Rocks (red sand-stone!)

golden sands

d u n e s

blockhouse

Northumberland Wildlife Trust Nature Reserve

'phone

Cheswick

golf course

golf club-house

Wind-swept trees at Sea House.

• Northumberland Wildlife Trust have a _Nature Reserve_ in the dune area behind Cocklawburn Beach. This section was once industrial, with local coal and limestone used to fuel the _limekilns_. Now it is a habitat for many lime-loving flowering plants. Visit in spring or summer if you can, for a colourful display.

Ruined limekiln, Cocklawburn.

25

Cheswick Links to the Causeway.

Cheswick Beach and the dune islands

* Walking south-east along the beach it is easy to miss the point where the actual shore-line turns south to Cheswick Golf Club, and Goswick. This is because the long bar of sand that stretches out towards Holy Island is quite high. Except when the tide is high you may not see over it if you follow the water's edge.

Ahead are two solitary tall dunes, capped with grass. These become islands at the top of the tide, as evidenced by the debris strewn over the sands. A lagoon then separates them from the shore.

According to tide, weather and your own whims you can decide where to cross to follow the main shoreline. (North Low appears to sink into the sands of the lagoon). You may wish to follow the beach along past Beachcomber House (with the lookout tower) — or go along the road past Goswick. This continues as a track and then as a public field-path. But the dunes separate it from all views of the sea.

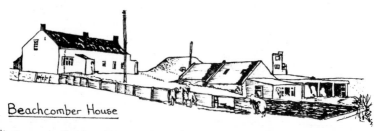

Beachcomber House

* Beyond the point you have an excellent view across the sands and/or water to Holy Island. Follow the shore path (or field path) south to meet and cross South Low (see the note opposite).

A squelchy path will take you on round Beal Point towards the Holy Island causeway. You approach the road by picking a route between huge concrete blocks, to reach the tide tables.

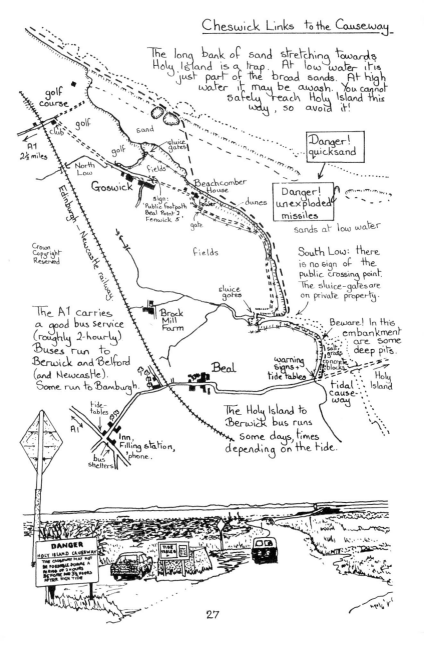

Cheswick Links to the Causeway

The long bank of sand stretching towards Holy Island is a trap. At low water it is just part of the broad sands. At high water it may be awash. You cannot safely reach Holy Island this way, so avoid it!

golf course

club

golf

A1 2½ miles

North Low

golf

sand

sluice gates

Goswick

fields

sign: 'Public Footpath Beal Point 2 Fenwick 5'

Beachcomber House

tower

dunes

gate

Danger! quicksand

Danger! unexploded missiles

sands at low water

Edinburgh – Newcastle railway

Crown Copyright Reserved

fields

South Low: there is no sign of the public crossing point. The sluice-gates are on private property.

sluice gates

Brock Mill Farm

The A1 carries a good bus service (roughly 2-hourly) Buses run to Berwick and Belford (and Newcastle). Some run to Bamburgh.

Beal

warning signs + tide tables

Beware! In this embankment are some deep pits.

salt grass

concrete blocks

Holy Island

tidal causeway

tide-tables

A1

Inn, Filling station, phone.

bus shelters

The Holy Island to Berwick bus runs some days, times depending on the tide.

DANGER
HOLY ISLAND CAUSEWAY
THE CAUSEWAY MAY NOT
BE PASSABLE DURING A
PERIOD OF 2 HOURS
BEFORE AND 3½ HOURS
AFTER HIGH TIDE

TIDE TABLE

27

Lindisfarne

The digression onto Holy Island is a must. Here is one of the ancient centres of British culture. Here during the Dark Ages Christianity took root. This little island had a reputation for learning throughout Europe.

Even if history bores you there is much to see on Lindisfarne.

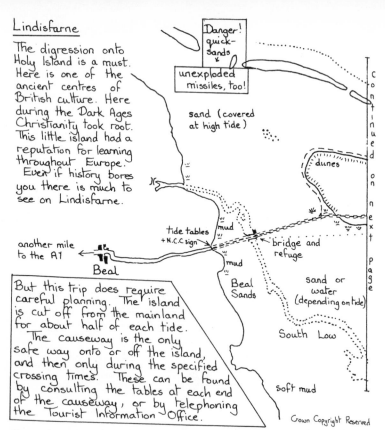

Danger! quick-sands ↓

unexploded missiles, too!

sand (covered at high tide)

dunes

tide tables + N.C.C sign

mud

bridge and refuge

mud

another mile to the A1

Beal

Beal Sands

sand or water (depending on tide)

South Low

soft mud

continued on next page

But this trip does require careful planning. The island is cut off from the mainland for about half of each tide.

The causeway is the only safe way onto or off the island, and then only during the specified crossing times. These can be found by consulting the tables at each end of the causeway, or by telephoning the Tourist Information Office.

Do make sure that you work out how long is available, whether you intend to be on the island and off again during one low-water period, or whether you plan to wait until the water drops again. Missing the tide, unplanned, can mean a long wait — and you may not fancy a crossing in the dark!

Every now and then someone disregards the timetable and gets caught on the causeway : the tide rises very fast, and runs strongly enough to push cars off the roadway: that's why the refuge box is there!

* Follow the causeway across to the Island, and along to the village. There you will find some shops catering for the tourist trade, selling the newly-traditional delights of Lindisfarne Liqueur, Lindisfarne Mead, Lindisfarne Fudge..., even a mead factory. There is also a Post Office and several public houses and hotels.

28

Holy Island

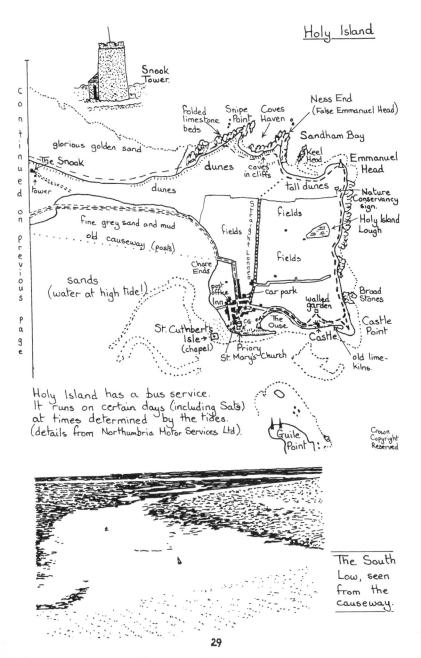

Snook Tower.

continued on previous page

Snipe Point
Folded limestone beds
Coves Haven
Ness End (False Emmanuel Head)
Sandham Bay
Keel Head
Emmanuel Head
glorious golden sand
The Snook
tower
dunes
caves in cliffs
dunes
tall dunes
Nature Conservancy sign.
Holy Island Lough
fine grey sand and mud
old causeway (posts)
fields
fields
Straight Lonnen
fields
fields
Chare Ends
sands (water at high tide!)
post office
Inn
car park
walled garden
Broad Stones
St. Cuthbert's Isle → (chapel)
C.G.
The Ouse
Castle
Castle Point
Priory
St. Mary's Church
old lime-kilns.

Holy Island has a bus service. It runs on certain days (including Sats) at times determined by the tides. (details from Northumbria Motor Services Ltd).

Guile Point

The South Low, seen from the causeway.

Lindisfarne Priory

The 'rainbow'

* The Priory is at the south end of the village, beyond the square.

Saint Aidan arrived on Lindisfarne in 635 AD, at the behest of Oswald, king of Northumbria. He established a Priory in the Celtic tradition which flourished, being esteemed throughout Europe. St. Cuthbert was Prior here, and Bishop of Lindisfarne.

The Priory lasted until 875, when the Danes burned it. Nothing material remains except the chapel ruins on St Cuthbert's Island. But still the island affects its visitors, many of who go away knowing just why it is called Holy Island.

● The ruins that you do see are of the later Priory. It was refounded by Benedictine monks from Durham Abbey in the 11th century. The architecture of the church is very similar to that of Durham Cathedral, with its carved alternating pillars. It was built at the same time. When complete it must have been a beautiful building, with Durham's form but rich red sandstone (from Cheswick). Even now it invokes awe.

The monastic buildings are later again (13th century), and are in a grey sandstone. The Priory was appropriated by Henry VIII, who had it stripped of roof and valuables. Even its stone went to build the castle.

● To the west of the Priory is the parish church of St Mary. This was established in 1140. It is worth a visit, as is the museum by the entrance to the Priory.

31

Lindisfarne: Priory to Castle

* From St Mary's go down the track towards St. Cuthbert's Island, and turn up to the left onto the Heugh.

• <u>St Cuthbert's Island</u> is semi-tidal. The ruins of the chapel there are the only remains of the Saxon Priory. St. Cuthbert used to seclude himself on the island (before resorting to the greater solitude of Inner Farne).

• <u>The Heugh</u> is a ridge of the Whin Sill (that is responsible for much of Northumberlands dramatic scenery). On the top is the Coastguard lookout. It has a fine view over the haven. To the south, on Guile Point, the Beacons are prominent.

* From the Heugh follow a path down past the fishermen's sheds, and pass their stores (made traditionally from upturned boats that have had their day.) Follow round the shore of the Ouse to the road, and follow that towards the castle.

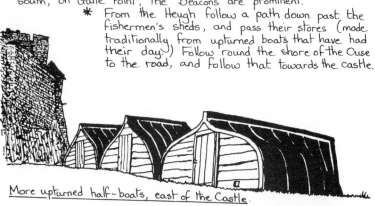

<u>More upturned half-boats, east of the Castle.</u>

- The <u>castle</u> is modern, by Northumbrian standards. A fort was established here around 1539, to guard the harbour. It held only a tiny garrison. Indeed, one day during the '15 two Jacobites found only two men on guard, and ousted them. They tried to flee, however, when troops arrived the next day.

  It was restored this century by Sir Edward Lutyens, to produce a romantic residence, perched atop a column of the Whin Sill. Now it is in the care of the National Trust.

- To the north is a <u>walled garden</u>, which is only open occasionally.

The castle seen from the Castle Garden.

The derelict lime-kilns, east of the Castle.

• The **kilns** are built against another basaltic pillar. You can see where the tramway ran, that brought limestone from the north side of the island to the kilns. (Coal came as a return trade for the lime – from Dundee).

* Beyond the kilns, venture out onto Castle Point. Out to sea the Farne Islands are prominent, with their light-houses: red + white on Longstone ; white on Inner Farne. Much more massive, Bamburgh Castle dominates the scene to the south, beyond the gold of Ross Back Sands.

* Follow the shore northwards towards Emmanuel Head. That white triangle is not a yacht's sail , but the large pyramidal day-mark on the head. You pass Holy Island Lough , which has whooper swans as winter visitors. The public footpath curves round past the Lough towards the dunes. As an alternative, use the shore to reach the Head.

From there you can look west over the series of rocky promontories that jut out from the island, and up the coast of the mainland towards Berwick.

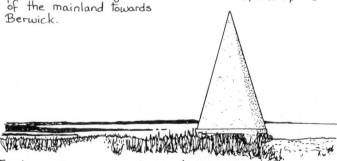

The day-mark on Emmanuel Head (about 30' high!)

Holy Island: Castle to Causeway

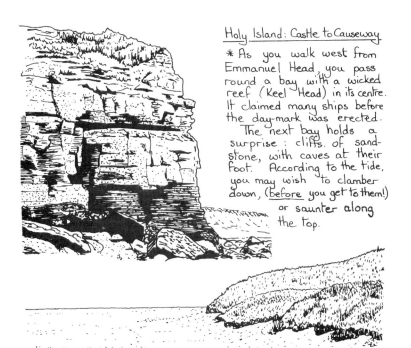

* As you walk west from Emmanuel Head, you pass round a bay with a wicked reef (Keel Head) in its centre. It claimed many ships before the day-mark was erected.

The next bay holds a surprise : cliffs. of sandstone, with caves at their foot. According to the tide, you may wish to clamber down, (<u>before</u> you get to them!) or saunter along the top.

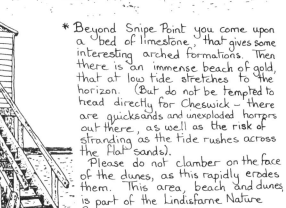

* Beyond Snipe Point you come upon a bed of limestone, that gives some interesting arched formations. Then there is an immense beach of gold, that at low tide stretches to the horizon. (But do not be tempted to head directly for Cheswick – there are quicksands and unexploded horrors out there, as well as the risk of stranding as the tide rushes across the flat sands).

Please do not clamber on the face of the dunes, as this rapidly erodes them. This area, beach and dunes, is part of the Lindisfarne Nature Reserve.

Go round the end of the island, to the causeway. Check that you have enough time before crossing. Remember the refuge!

Lindisfarne Nature Reserve

• The Nature Conservancy Council manage the Nature Reserve comprising part of Holy Island and a vast inter-tidal area stretching down to Budle Bay. As this is below the high tide level, and there is no public footpath behind the beach in most places, visits must be carefully planned to avoid trespass.

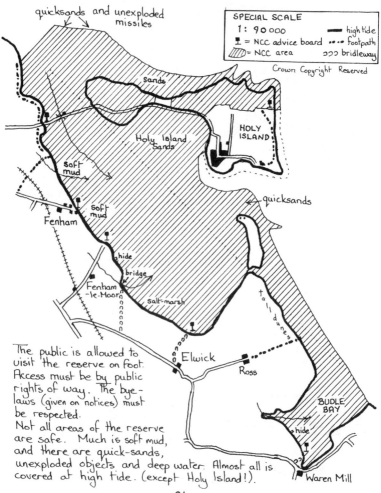

quicksands and unexploded missiles

SPECIAL SCALE
1 : 90 000
⚑ = NCC advice board
▨ = NCC area
━━ high tide
•••• footpath
ↄↄↄ bridleway

Crown Copyright Reserved

sands

HOLY ISLAND

Holy Island Sands

soft mud

← quicksands

Fenham

soft mud

hide

bridge

Fenham-le-Moor

salt-marsh

tall dunes

Elwick

Ross

BUDLE BAY

hide

Waren Mill

The public is allowed to visit the reserve on foot. Access must be by public rights of way. The bye-laws (given on notices) must be respected.

Not all areas of the reserve are safe. Much is soft mud, and there are quick-sands, unexploded objects and deep water. Almost all is covered at high tide. (except Holy Island!).

36

Fenham (NOT in the Reserve!)

The reserve is best known for the variety of its wildfowl and wading birds. There are residents, winter visitors and passing migrants. Take a pair of binoculars and a bird book, and listen too — the lovely liquid call of the curlew is often to be heard over the Flats. Take your time, but remember the tide and your planned point of egress.

More information about the Reserve may be obtained from:

Regional Officer
Nature Conservancy Council
Archbold House
Archbold Terrace
NEWCASTLE upon TYNE
NE2 1EG

A hide overlooking Fenham Flats.

Holy Island Causeway to Elwick Shore

I expected this to be straightforward. Even though there is a distinct lack of public paths above the tide-line for most of the way, the inter-tidal zone offers open access. But Black Low proved to be impassable at the shore, and soft mud may prevent progress past Fenham. Diversions inland using rights of way may have to be used:

* From the causeway head southwards, following a soggy path between the twin lines of concrete blocks. A stile marks the start of the path up onto Fenham Hill. Follow a succession of stiles and gates to the railway. Make sure that nothing is hurtling towards you at high speed, and cross the tracks. (The ballast is very wide, as the curve has been flattened. The cant of the tracks is to allow very high speeds despite the curve.)

Follow the hedge up the hill to a lane. Here you have a choice:
- the simple route goes right briefly, then follows the lane past Fenwick Granary to the A1. If you prefer less of the main road then follow the lane downhill to Fenham.

Beyond the farm (with its attractive trees), you pass a cluster of houses with well-kept gardens, and a field of grassy mounds. (There is a story under there somewhere). A narrow alley leads down to the shore. But the mud is deep, soft and sticky!

A field-path heads inland again, from just north of the farm. It goes past a prominent electricity pole, to another crossing of the railway. (I hope you enjoy train-spotting). The burn beyond is more of a problem in wet weather. Go on up the slope by the hedge, towards Fenwick Stead. At a belt of derelict trees, head up to the left of the farm-buildings. A lane takes you towards the A1, but you can go straight on at a corner, to the right of a hedge, up to a hidden stile onto the main road.

Fortunately there is a wide verge, with a rudimentary path in the grass, for the short walk past Buckton to the next seaward lane. Enjoy the extensive views, right over Holy Island. Even the beacon on Emmanuel Head may be seen. Go downhill again, over Lowmoor Crossing. Watch for the birds in the hedgerows – a popular roost for migrants.

Beyond Fenham-le-Moor you reach a beach. Real sand! Follow it south round Tealhole Point. On the way you will pass a "hide" – up on stilts, as it is below the high water mark. A footbridge takes you over Fenham Burn. Turn down the steps to the shore below the field embankment.

Follow the edge of the salt-marsh southwards, below the raised fields, towards Elwick Shore. The reed-like grass that clogs the upper beach is Spartina. This collects silt on the tide, and was deliberately introduced here to build up the land. It competed with the native Eel Grass, that is essential to the Brent geese, and consequently has had to be controlled.

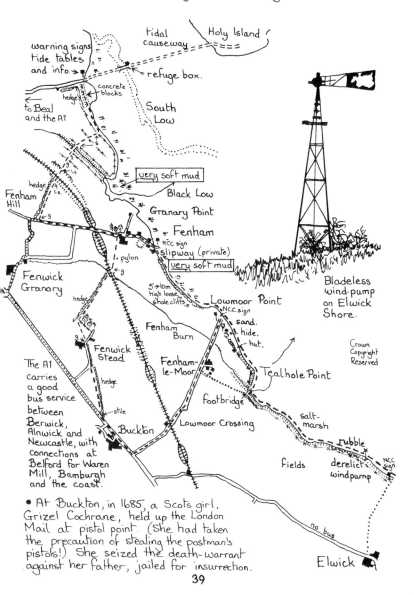

tidal causeway

Holy Island

warning signs
tide tables
and info →

refuge box.

concrete blocks

hedge

to Beal and the A1

South Low

Fenham Hill

hedge l.s.

very soft mud

Black Low

Granary Point

Fenham

NCC sign

slipway (private)

very soft mud

Fenwick Granary

pylon

hedge

5→10m high loose shale cliffs

Lowmoor Point

NCC sign

sand.

hide.

hut.

Fenham Burn

Fenwick Stead

Fenham-le-Moor

Tealhole Point

The A1 carries a good bus service between Berwick, Alnwick and Newcastle, with connections at Belford for Waren Mill, Bamburgh and the coast.

hedge

stile

Buckton

footbridge

Lowmoor Crossing

salt-marsh

rubble

Fields

derelict windpump

NCC sign

no bus

Elwick

Bladeless wind-pump on Elwick Shore.

• At Buckton, in 1685, a Scots girl, Grizel Cochrane, held up the London Mail at pistol point. (She had taken the precaution of stealing the postman's pistols!) She seized the death-warrant against her father, jailed for insurrection.

39

Elwick Shore to Ross Back Sands

The Beacons on Guile Point

* From Elwick Shore the coast curves gently round towards Guile Point. Behind the embankment on the right are the low fields of Ross Farm, jealously guarded against the high tide. The farm is protected on the seaward side by 20 metre high dunes, whilst long lines of conifers combat the wind. Underfoot the *Spartina* gives way to sand.

At the gap separating off Old Law you should consider time and tide. The sea runs through here as high tide approaches, making Old Law an island. If your timing is right, continue along the soft sandy shore to the Beacons. Enjoy the broad views over the Flats with the Kyloe Hills beyond — and a glimpse of the Cheviots too. Watch too for the wildfowl (and, in their season, wildfowlers too). Lindisfarne comes back into view as you round Guile Point, with the Heugh and the Castle most prominent. But do not be tempted to head out across the sands at low tide: there are quicksands!

* Now follow the sea-shore southwards. Here is typical Northumberland coastal scenery: tall dunes and broad sands. Recross the gap at Ross Point, and continue along the shore. Ahead of you now is Bamburgh Castle, and out to sea the Farne Islands.

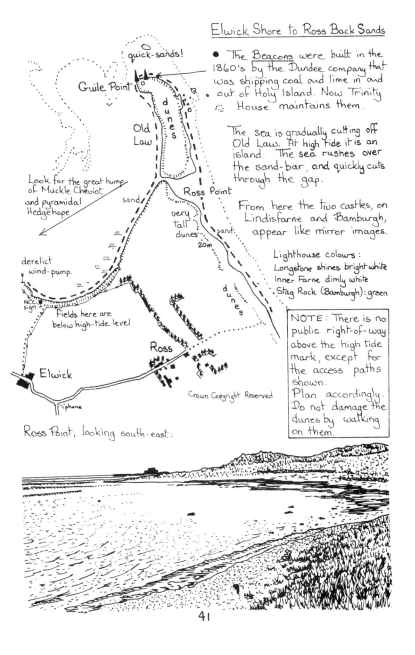

Elwick Shore to Ross Back Sands

quick-sands!

Guile Point

Old Law

dunes

Look for the great hump of Muckle Cheviot, and pyramidal Hedgehope

sand

Ross Point

very tall dunes

20m

dunes

derelict wind-pump.

NCC sign

fields here are below high-tide level

Ross

Elwick

phone

Crown Copyright Reserved

• The **Beacons** were built in the 1860's by the Dundee company that was shipping coal and lime in and out of Holy Island. Now Trinity House maintains them.

The sea is gradually cutting off Old Law. At high tide it is an island. The sea rushes over the sand-bar, and quickly cuts through the gap.

From here the two castles, on Lindisfarne and Bamburgh, appear like mirror images.

Lighthouse colours :
Longstone shines bright white
Inner Farne dimly white
Stag Rock (Bamburgh): green

NOTE: There is no public right-of-way above the high tide mark, except for the access paths shown.
Plan accordingly.
Do not damage the dunes by walking on them.

Ross Point, looking south-east:

41

Wreck of a cement-laden barge on the sand-spit, Budle Bay

Budle Bay poses problems:

① The mouth of the bay, although narrow at low tide, is deep and dangerous. Lives have been lost here. Do NOT attempt to cross.

② Ross Low can be waded, with care, when the tide is out (and not after rain). But you need a taste for mud — of the ankle-deep, boot-sucking variety. Wellies are called for!

③ There is no right of way above the high tide mark. If the tide is in, or the river swollen, you cannot pass without trespass. So use the other, inland route, on the public footpath across Ross Links, and the lanes via Ross and Eastington.

＊ So before setting off from the post on Ross Links, or Waren Mill, consider the state of the tide, weather and footwear.

Budle Bay itself is quite fascinating: a spit of firm sand runs south almost to Black Rock below Budle Point. This spit is a favourite roost for sea-birds as the tide comes in. Two wrecks lie half-buried in sand.

Inland, the summits of Cheviot and Hedgehope peep over the Kyloe hills.

Hide near Waren Mill

42

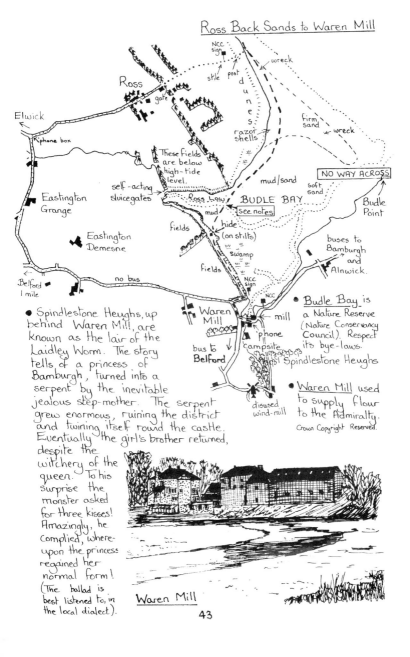

NCC
sign

stile post
d
u
n
e
s

wreck

Ross

gate

Elwick

phone box

These fields
are below
high-tide
level.

razor
shells

firm
sand   wreck

self-acting
sluice gates

mud/sand

NO WAY ACROSS

Eastington
Grange

Ross Low

soft
sand

Budle
Point

BUDLE BAY

See notes

Eastington
Demesne

fields

mud

hide
(on stilts)

buses to
Bamburgh
and
Alnwick.

swamp

fields

Belford
1 mile   no bus

NCC
sign

NCC

Waren
Mill   mill

bus to
Belford

phone

campsite

disused
wind-mill

Spindlestone Heughs

• **Budle Bay** is
a Nature Reserve
(Nature Conservancy
Council). Respect
its bye-laws.

• **Waren Mill** used
to supply flour
to the Admiralty.
Crown Copyright Reserved.

• Spindlestone Heughs, up
behind Waren Mill, are
known as the lair of the
Laidley Worm. The story
tells of a princess of
Bamburgh, turned into a
serpent by the inevitable
jealous step-mother. The serpent
grew enormous, ruining the district
and twining itself round the castle.
Eventually the girl's brother returned,
despite the
witchery of the
queen. To his
surprise the
monster asked
for three kisses!
Amazingly, he
complied, where-
upon the princess
regained her
normal form!
(The ballad is
best listened to, in
the local dialect).

Waren Mill

43

Waren Mill to Bamburgh.

Budle Point

Waren Mill still has the mill-buildings, as well as a large sheltered camp-site (that has a shop and other amenities). There are buses to Belford and Berwick, and the other way, to Bamburgh.

* From the mill follow the road alongside Budle Bay. A pair of binoculars and a bird-book are distinct assets here, as the bay supports huge numbers of birds as residents or visitors. Greylag geese and waders invade Chesterhill Slakes in winter, and large numbers of birds gather on the sands opposite.

At Budle, turn north down the track to the sea past some cottages. Enter the National Nature Reserve (note the sign), and turn east along the shore. The beach soon turns from stones to very fine sand. Pass Heather Cottages and the old quay (once a loading point for whinstone quarried from Kittling Hill). Continue along the beach to Black Rock, a large flat slab of dolerite that marks the end of Budle Bay.

The view north and west from Black Point is extensive, with Ross Links and Holy Island to the north, and the Kyloe Hills forming a backdrop to the glistening expanse of Budle Bay.

More sand, and mixed outcrops of rock below low cliffs are met on the way to Stag Point. A path leads up past the automatic lighthouse. Beyond, the rocky shoreline can be followed over Harkess Rocks, and on to the sandy beach, or the road can be followed into Bamburgh Village. The castle on its dolerite mound dominates the view (unless it is foggy!).

If the sea is angry or the tide very high, you may wish to use another route, from Heather Cottages, over Kittling Hill to the golf club-house, and then the road.

44

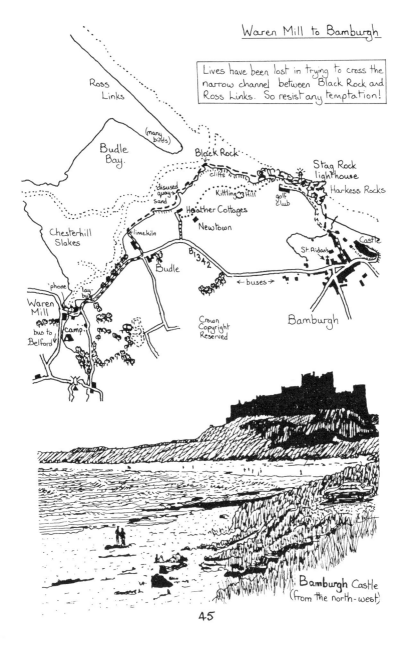

Lives have been lost in trying to cross the narrow channel between Black Rock and Ross Links. So resist any temptation!

Ross Links

Budle Bay.

(many birds)

Black Rock

Stag Rock lighthouse

Harkess Rocks

cliffs

disused quay·sand

Kittling

golf club

Heather Cottages

Newtown

Chesterhill Slakes

limekiln

B1342

St Aidans

Castle

phone

lay·by

Budle

← buses →

Waren Mill

bus to Belford

camp.

Bamburgh

Crown Copyright Reserved

Bamburgh Castle (from the north-west)

45

Bamburgh.

• <u>Bamburgh</u> is not just a castle, although the massive edifice does dominate the village. The latter caters for holiday-makers, and has accommodation, a coffee-house, gift-shops.....

In the centre is a patch of green — a clump of trees. There are many worse places than Bamburgh to wait for a bus.

These run west to Belford, and then Berwick (by connection or direct); or south to Seahouses, Embleton, Craster, Alnwick and Newcastle.

The Castle from the beach.

Bamburgh Castle

- The great 40m high block of basalt, overlooking the sea has been fortified since AD 547, when Ida, King of Northumbria, raised a wooden fortress surrounded by a hedge. His grandson, King Ethelfrith, gave it to his wife Bebba, giving rise to the name Bebbanburgh.

  The Viking raids wrought destruction on the fortress, but Henry I rebuilt it, adding the huge stone keep. It stayed in royal hands, and had an active history in the border wars. Here kings of England and Scotland met. Here queens were beseiged and held their court. Queen Margaret, wife of Henry VI, used this as her fortress during the Wars of the Roses, until she rode from here to fight, and lose, the Battle of Hexham.

  Eventually James I gave it away, to the Forsters of Addlestone, wardens of the Eastern March, who hung onto it for an hundred years.

  Lord Crewe, bishop of Durham, who married Dorothy Forster, bought it in 1704, and began the work of restoring the castle, that had succumbed to the ravages of gunpowder and artillery. He established a trust for the work, so that it continued after his death (He also established other charity trusts, that still exist today).

  Lord Armstrong, the Tyneside inventor, eventually bought it and "improved" it to its present condition.

- The castle is still a residence, being divided into apartments, but is open to the public.

  Access is by the long drive that winds up past the southern aspect to a high gateway on the eastern flank.

  The battlements provide a magnificent viewpoint when the air is clear Close offshore the Farne Islands attract the attention. Resolve to visit them.

Saint Aidan's Church.

- Saint Aidan's church is a lovely place. It dates from the 13th century, replacing the previous building established for Aidan. It is a large church for a tiny village. Sit inside and ponder on the faith that produced it. The stained glass commemorates the saints of Northumbria. Outside, the memorial is a Victorian tribute to Grace Darling.

The gatehouse of Bamburgh Castle - probably originally Norman, but 'restored'. Over the wall on the right is one of the best panoramas in the land.

Grace Darling.

Bamburgh

was the daughter of the lighthouse-keeper on Longstone, one of the Farne Islands. In the early light of 7th September 1838, when she was 23 years old, Grace was on watch during a gale. She saw a vessel (the 'Forfarshire') strike Big Harcar, and alerted her father. A little later (7a.m.) they spotted survivors on the rock. They decided that although they could not hope to row both ways in the wind, that survivors might be able to help them to row back. They launched their coble, and found eight men and a woman on the rock (out of fifty-two on the vessel). They could not carry all of them, so took five to start with. Two of the survivors helped them to make a second trip, saving all nine.

The event made the Darlings national heroes, and Grace refused several offers of marriage to stay at the light. Unfortunately, she died of consumption only four years later, despite kindness and hospitality from the Duchess of Northumberland.

• A large ornate <u>memorial</u> stands near the church door at Saint Aidan's, within sight of the sea. There is also in Bamburgh a museum of Grace Darling memorabilia, with the famous coble. More importantly, the public outcry resulted in better inspections for ships. All sailors have cause to be thankful to Grace Darling.

Grace Darling
Memorial.
(without the
railings!)

Bamburgh to Seahouses

A gap in the dunes reveals the Farne Islands, beyond the Islestone.

- <u>Seahouses</u>: here in summer you will find fish and chips, candy floss, oversized lollipops and 'kiss-me-quick' hats.
  Meals and accommodation are available, and there is car-parking and an Information Centre. Shops, too!
- Not to be missed: (a) <u>the harbour</u>, with its colourful cobles, (b) <u>a trip to the Farne Islands</u>.

<u>Seahouses</u>

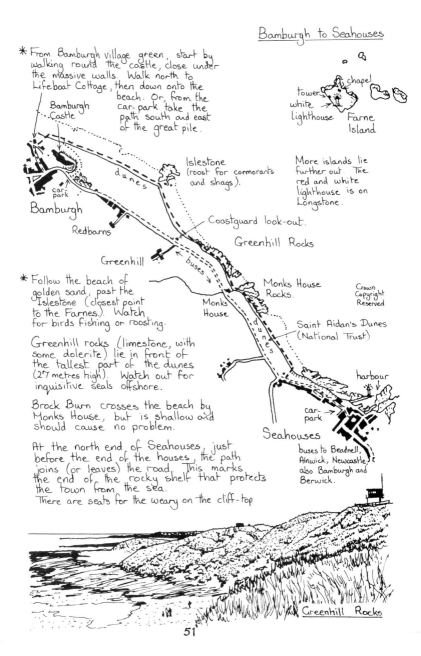

* From Bamburgh village green, start by walking round the castle, close under the massive walls. Walk north to Lifeboat Cottage, then down onto the beach. Or, from the car-park take the path south and east of the great pile.

Bamburgh Castle

Bamburgh

car-park

Redbarns

Greenhill

* Follow the beach of golden sand, past the Islestone (closest point to the Farnes.) Watch for birds fishing or roosting.

Greenhill rocks (limestone, with some dolerite) lie in front of the tallest part of the dunes (2·7 metres high). Watch out for inquisitive seals offshore.

Brock Burn crosses the beach by Monks House, but is shallow and should cause no problem.

At the north end of Seahouses, just before the end of the houses, the path joins (or leaves) the road. This marks the end of the rocky shelf that protects the town from the sea.
There are seats for the weary on the cliff-top

dunes

Islestone (roost for cormorants and shags).

Coastguard look-out.

Greenhill Rocks

buses

Monks House Rocks.

Monks House

dunes

Saint Aidan's Dunes (National Trust)

chapel

tower
white lighthouse

Farne Island

More islands lie further out. The red and white lighthouse is on Longstone.

Crown Copyright Reserved

harbour

car-park

Seahouses

buses to Beadnell, Alnwick, Newcastle, also Bamburgh and Berwick.

Greenhill Rocks

51

The Farne Islands

If the weather is clear, you cannot fail to notice them as you walk the coast. They are the easternmost outcrop of the Great Whin Sill, the hard basalt resisting erosion by the sea to leave a scattered group of islands over an area 4km by 3km.

Two have lighthouses: Inner Farne (white) and Longstone (red and white). The former is 2½ km from the mainland, and the latter 6½ km, but both appear much closer on a good day.

The islands are host to a vast number of sea-birds: here there are waders all year round — turnstones, dunlin, purple sandpipers. Seabirds come here to breed. You may see cormorants and shags; fulmars, kittiwakes and gulls; eider ducks and terns; guillemots, razor-bills and little auks, plus thousands of puffins. There are ringed plover, oyster catchers and rock pipits each year, plus occasional pairs of other birds. In addition, hundreds of <u>kinds</u> of bird pass through here each year during migration.

The islands have been a bird sanctuary for over a century, but long before that St. Cuthbert had a special affection for eiders, that are still known on this coast as Cuddy's ducks.

Seals colonise the islands, and can be seen curiously inspecting the passing boat-loads of people. In November the pups are born, mainly on the Wamses and the Northern Hares (north of Longstone). Within a few weeks the young seals are weaned and scattered across the northern oceans.

Rabbits also breed on the islands, and compete for burrow-space with the puffins.

Casual human visitors are allowed to land only on Inner Farne (on payment of a landing fee), where they can visit the chapel. Hermits and monks lived on the island during a period of nearly 900 years. Most remembered is St. Cuthbert, the holy man whose influence affected the church in Northern Britain for some centuries, and whose tomb is in a place of honour in Durham Cathedral.

Boat-trips round the islands are available (in suitable weather) from Seahouses Harbour. Remember to take the landing fee for Inner Farne, and a good pair of binoculars.

A good bird-book is a sensible preparation too.

The National Trust publish their own guide "Farne Islands", that gives much useful information in an attractive way.

The boat-landing, Inner Farne.

• Boat trips from Seahouses take you round the islands, giving you close views of the nesting and roosting birds, and the seals if there. A brief landing is usually on the itinerary – on Inner Farne of course. You can visit the chapel and walk round the island.

Cormorants on Staple Island

Seahouses to Beadnell

Braidcarr Rocks,
Snook Point.

Beadnell Haven

Seahouses to Beadnell.

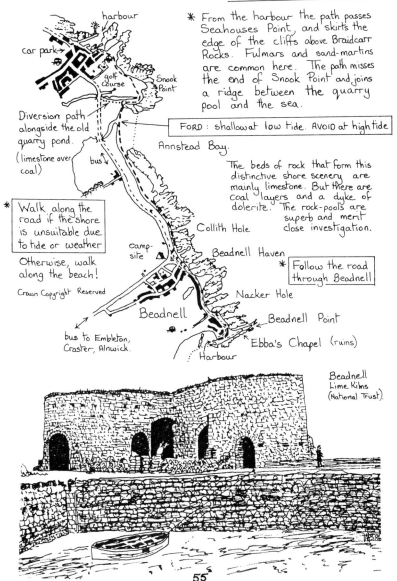

* From the harbour the path passes Seahouses Point, and skirts the edge of the cliffs above Braidcarr Rocks. Fulmars and sand-martins are common here. The path misses the end of Snook Point and joins a ridge between the quarry pool and the sea.

FORD: shallow at low tide. AVOID at high tide

Annstead Bay.

The beds of rock that form this distinctive shore scenery are mainly limestone. But there are coal layers and a dyke of dolerite. The rock-pools are superb and merit close investigation.

* Follow the road through Beadnell

harbour

car park →

golf course

Snook Point

Diversion path alongside the old quarry pond.
(limestone over coal)

bus

* Walk along the road if the shore is unsuitable due to tide or weather

Otherwise, walk along the beach!

camp-site △

Collith Hole

Beadnell Haven

Nacker Hole

Beadnell

bus to Embleton, Craster, Alnwick.

Beadnell Point

Ebba's Chapel (ruins)

Harbour

Beadnell Lime Kilns (National Trust).

55

Beadnell

- Beadnell has two centres: the minuscule harbour and the old village. The <u>harbour</u>, dry at low tide, has massive stone piers, matched in style and solidity by the <u>lime-kilns</u> on the quay. Nowadays they are used to store lobster-pots and fish boxes, and are in the care of the National Trust. The old loading ramp up to the top of the kilns can be followed on the north-east side.
- Very little remains of <u>Ebba's Chapel</u> on the long narrow Beadnell Point (also known as Ebba's Snook) — but it is an excellent view-point. (Bamburgh Castle, Dunstanburgh, and the Farne Islands feature in the view on a good day). A path leads out onto the point on the south (seaward) side of the houses.

The village has a beautiful church (St. Ebba's), and an inn, the Craster Arms, built round a Pele Tower. There are also a camp-site and caravan sites.

The rocky shore by the village yields hundreds of rock-pools, with their fascinating fauna: little crabs, hermit crabs, snails, sea anemones, tiny fish....

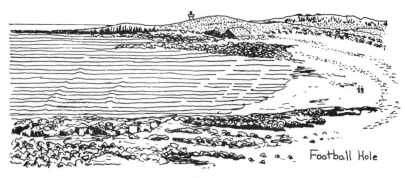

Football Hole

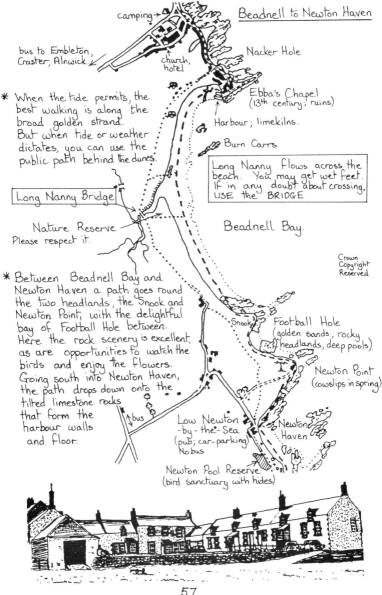

Beadnell to Newton Haven

camping →

bus to Embleton, Craster, Alnwick ↙

church, hotel

Nacker Hole

Ebba's Chapel (13th century; ruins)

Harbour; limekilns.

Burn Carrs.

* When the tide permits, the best walking is along the broad golden strand. But when tide or weather dictates, you can use the public path behind the dunes.

Long Nanny Bridge

Nature Reserve — Please respect it.

Long Nanny flows across the beach. You may get wet feet. If in any doubt about crossing, USE the BRIDGE

Beadnell Bay.

Crown Copyright Reserved

* Between Beadnell Bay and Newton Haven a path goes round the two headlands, the Snook and Newton Point, with the delightful bay of Football Hole between. Here the rock scenery is excellent, as are opportunities to watch the birds and enjoy the flowers. Going south into Newton Haven, the path drops down onto the tilted limestone rocks that form the harbour walls and floor.

Snook

Football Hole (golden sands, rocky headlands, deep pools).

Newton Point (cowslips in spring)

↑ bus

Low Newton -by-the-Sea (pub; car-parking) No bus

Newton Haven

Newton Pool Reserve (bird sanctuary with hides)

57

Embleton Bay : the view to Dunstanburgh Castle from Low Newton-by-the-Sea

Newton Haven to Dunstanburgh Castle

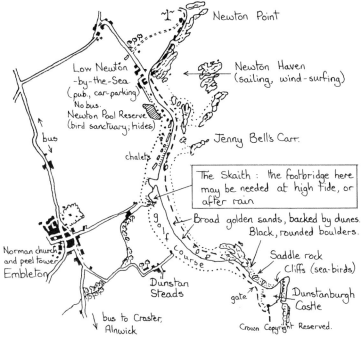

Newton Point

Newton Haven
(sailing, wind-surfing)

Low Newton
-by-the-Sea.
(pub., car-parking)
No bus.
Newton Pool Reserve
(bird sanctuary; hides)

bus

chalets

Jenny Bell's Carr.

The Skaith : the footbridge here
may be needed at high tide, or
after rain

Broad golden sands, backed by dunes.
Black, rounded boulders.

golf course

Saddle rock
Cliffs (sea-birds)

gate

Dunstanburgh
Castle

Norman church
and peel tower.
Embleton

Dunstan
Steads

bus to Craster,
Alnwick

Crown Copyright Reserved.

* The broad beach is the best place to travel round Embleton Bay.
But there is a parallel public footpath through the dunes, that
offers a foul-weather alternative (or a return route).
Note the availability of the footbridge over the Skaith.
Do NOT attempt to walk around the Dunstanburgh headland,
at sea-level! But do use your binoculars to observe the
gulls nesting or roosting on the dramatic black cliffs.

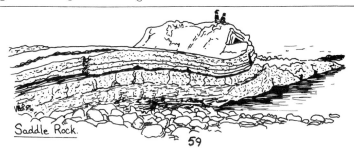

Saddle Rock.

59

Dunstanburgh Castle

Lilburn Tower

• Despite its grandeur and its impressive location, <u>Dunstanburgh Castle</u> has played only a brief and minor rôle in national events. It was built late. Thomas, Earl of Lancaster had it built as a secure refuge, starting in 1313 (he was executed for treason in 1322). Sir John Lilburn became constable, and had the Lilburn Tower built, around 1325. John of Gaunt, when Lieutenant of the Scottish Marches built another gateway in about 1380, the massive gatehouse being walled up as a keep.

During the Wars of the Roses the castle changed hands several times. Queen Margaret is reputed to have stayed here after the Battle of Hexham before taking ship from the cove below. But the development of artillery rendered the castle redundant, and from 1464, after only 140 years use, the castle fell into disrepair. By 1550 it was considered a ruin.

It is a remarkable tribute to its builders that so much remains standing after 500 years of neglect. Now it is in the hands of English Heritage, who charge an admission fee and have useful guides to the castle and its wildlife. They also have postcards!

Dunstanburgh Castle

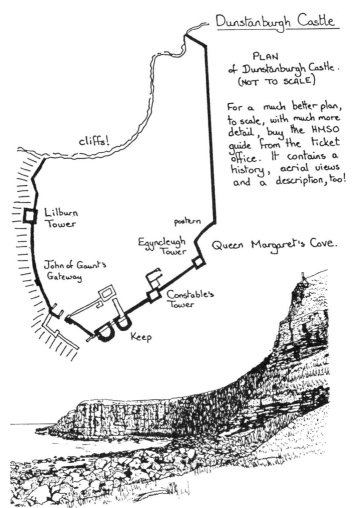

PLAN
of Dunstanburgh Castle.
(NOT TO SCALE)

For a much better plan, to scale, with much more detail, buy the HMSO guide from the ticket office. It contains a history, aerial views and a description, too!

cliffs!

Lilburn Tower

postern

Egyncleugh Tower

Queen Margaret's Cove.

John of Gaunt's Gateway

Constable's Tower

Keep

The designers of the castle selected a site that offers superb natural protection. The great Bailey occupies the top of an outcrop of the Great Whin Sill. (This is the basalt that appears throughout Northumbria: High Force tumbles down over it; Hadrian's Wall strides along it; Bamburgh and Dunstanburgh Castles perch atop it.) As a result, no walls at all are required on the north side.

Dunstanburgh

The Keep.

* From the Castle gate follow the track southwards, gently descending towards the rocky promontory of Cushat Stiel. Continue on the path as it veers right, dropping down through a rim of rocks to pass the little bay of Nova Scotia. Now you can walk on fine turf all the way to Craster, or you could digress onto the rocky foreshore.

John of Gaunt's Gateway

Lilburn Tower

The Keep (original gate)

Constable's Tower

Egyncleugh Tower

Dunstanburgh Castle to Craster

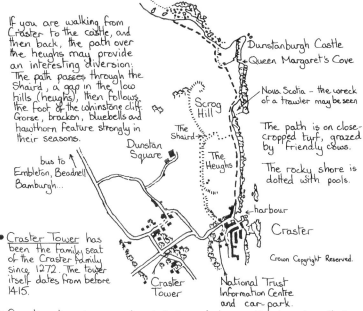

If you are walking from Craster to the castle, and then back, the path over the heughs may provide an interesting diversion: The path passes through the Shaird, a gap in the low hills (heughs), then follows the foot of the whinstone cliff. Gorse, bracken, bluebells and hawthorn feature strongly in their seasons.

bus to Embleton, Beadnell, Bamburgh...

Dunstanburgh Castle
Queen Margaret's Cove
Nova Scotia - the wreck of a trawler may be seen

The path is on close-cropped turf, grazed by friendly cows.

The rocky shore is dotted with pools.

Scrog Hill
The Shaird
The Heughs
Dunstan Square

harbour

Craster

Crown Copyright Reserved.

- <u>Craster Tower</u> has been the family seat of the Craster family since 1272. The tower itself dates from before 1415.

Craster Tower

National Trust Information Centre and car-park.

- <u>Craster</u> lies in a natural hollow between the heughs, that afford it shelter from north and south (unlike most villages on the Northumberland coast, that have exposed locations).
  The natural harbour is reinforced by two massive jetties. Whinstone from the quarry used to be exported from here.
  Fishing cobles still venture out for lobsters and herring. Kippers are a Craster speciality, with a wide reputation. Buses for both coastal directions come into the village to turn round. Car-parking is available (for a small fee) at the quarry, where there is also a National Trust information Centre and a Nature Reserve.

Craster Harbour

Craster to Howick

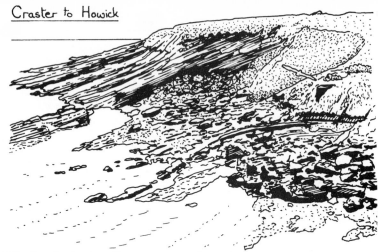

• South of Craster the raw bones of the land lie exposed: Long Heugh, ending in Cullernose Point, is of dolerite, hard and columnar. Swine Den, the little bay south of the point, is floored with round whinstone boulders. Next come great folds of grey limestone, arched and twisted by geological pressures. Yellow sandstones make up the cliffs beyond. Explore the beach, and look at the fascinating skeleton of strata revealed.

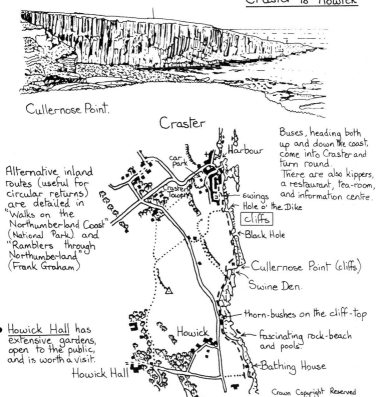

Cullernose Point.

Craster

Buses, heading both up and down the coast, come into Craster and turn round.
There are also kippers, a restaurant, tea-room, and information centre.

Alternative inland routes (useful for circular returns) are detailed in "Walks on the Northumberland Coast" (National Park). and "Ramblers through Northumberland" (Frank Graham)

car park

Harbour

Craster Tower

swings

Hole o' the Dyke

cliffs

Black Hole

Cullernose Point (cliffs)

Swine Den.

thorn-bushes on the cliff-top

Howick

fascinating rock-beach and pools.

• Howick Hall has extensive gardens, open to the public, and is worth a visit.

Howick Hall

Bathing House

Crown Copyright Reserved

* The coast-walk leaves Craster beyond the children's play-park. Follow the cliff past the school, then jink abruptly round 'Hole o' the Dyke, and continue along the cliffs. Pass the sinister-sounding Black Hole to the heights of Cullernose Point. When the tide is out, the view is spectacular, revealing the strata of rock that underlie the bay to the south. Turn down to the west, and follow the path south. Look back at the face of the cliffs, and note the smoothly folded limestone closer to hand. The path climbs up to meet the narrow lane. Thorn bushes, with paths half-buried in them, occupy the space between lane and cliff. After a few hundred metres or so the path veers off to follow the cliffs again. Now these are negotiable in places, so that with care you can pick a grassy route down to the beach, if you wish to look at the rocks, picnic, sunbathe .... The path continues along the top to the bathing-house near Rumbling Kern.

Howick Hall

• <u>Howick Hall</u> is the home of the Grey family.   The Hall was
built in 1782 to a design by William Newton of Newcastle,
on a site that had been occupied by a tower since before 1416.
Just across the burn to the south is the <u>church</u>, dating from 1746.
The <u>gardens</u> are extensive, attractive and informative.   They
are open to the public on spring and summer afternoons. A
visit when the grounds are swathed in daffodils, with the
first rhododendrons bursting into bloom and the buds breaking
on the trees, will never be forgotten.   The <u>Silver Wood</u>
is a marvelous woodland of beech with elms and conifers.
A <u>woodland walk</u> crosses the public road by a bridge, and
continues down beside Howick Burn to the sea. Behind the
beach the woods are carpeted with unusual double-bloom
daffodils.

Howick Hall

Silver Wood

Howick to Boulmer

● Rumbling Kern is just south of the bathing house. It is a large hole in the rocks, through which the sea sucks and surges. There are superb sheltered spots on the beaches and rocks. Enjoy the rock-pools, and the interesting rock formations.

* From the bathing house there is a choice of routes to the bridge over Howick Burn: — the beach is best, if the tide permits; — the cliff path is badly eroded and is not recommended; — a sign-posted alternative route goes inland to the road corner, then south to reach the footbridge.

The route continues either along the shore or the cliff-path above. There is a succession of delightful bays and magnificent rocks, all the way to Boulmer.

Part of boiler from the French trawler 'Tadorne'

The bathing house, Howick

Howick Hall
(The gardens and woodland walk to the sea are private. The public is admitted during spring and summer afternoons, for a small fee).

buses to Craster...
↑ buses to Craster
bathing house
Howick SeaHouses
Rumbling Kern
Howick Haven
mineral springs in cliffs.
part of wrecked ship's boiler.
bridge
Iron Scars
Sugar Sands
bridge over road
crumbly cliffs signs
buses to Alnwick...
primroses and cowslips.
Howdiemont Sands
Longhoughton Steel
car park
Crown Copyright Reserved

• <u>The bathing house</u> was built for the Grey Family in Victorian times. Just below it is a rectangular pool, with iron hooks and socket holes in the rock, presumably for tents or awnings.

• <u>RAF Boulmer</u> is the base for the Rescue helicopters.

Boulmer

Bewick Stone.
'Fishing Boat'

toilets
Life-boat station
Post Office

infrequent buses to Alnmouth, Alnwick ↓

bus shelter

Boulmer Haven

RAF RESCUE

Boulmer

- Boulmer has a long tradition of smuggling. Some of the houses are reputed to have hidden cellars, once used for caching rum and other contraband. The 'Fishing Boat' Inn has been associated with the 'free trade'.

The Haven is almost enclosed by a ring of rocks, that break up the seas that pound the coast. The narrow gap to provide access is marked from the shore by the two leading marks (right).

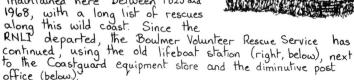

Boulmer also has a tradition of life-saving. A lifeboat was maintained here between 1825 and 1968, with a long list of rescues along this wild coast. Since the RNLI departed, the Boulmer Volunteer Rescue Service has continued, using the old lifeboat station (right, below), next to the Coastguard equipment store and the diminutive post office (below.).

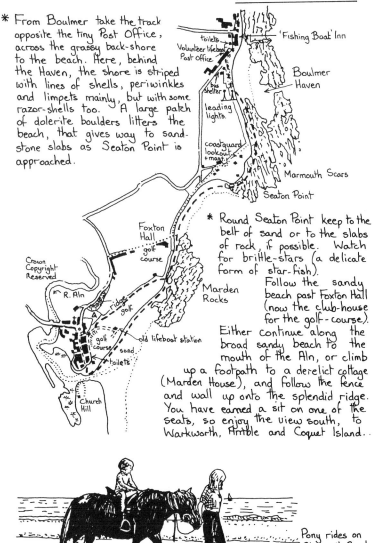

* From Boulmer take the track opposite the tiny Post Office, across the grassy back-shore to the beach. Here, behind the Haven, the shore is striped with lines of shells, periwinkles and limpets mainly, but with some razor-shells too. A large patch of dolerite boulders litters the beach, that gives way to sand-stone slabs as Seaton Point is approached.

* Round Seaton Point keep to the belt of sand or to the slabs of rock, if possible. Watch for brittle-stars (a delicate form of star-fish).

Follow the sandy beach past Foxton Hall (now the club-house for the golf-course).

Either continue along the broad sandy beach to the mouth of the Aln, or climb up a footpath to a derelict cottage (Marden House), and follow the fence and wall up onto the splendid ridge. You have earned a sit on one of the seats, so enjoy the view south, to Warkworth, Amble and Coquet Island..

'Fishing Boat' Inn
toilets
Volunteer lifeboat
Post Office
Boulmer Haven
bus shelter
leading lights
coastguard lookout + mast
Marmouth Scars
Seaton Point
Foxton Hall
golf course
Crown Copyright Reserved
R. Aln
ridge golf
Marden Rocks
golf course
old lifeboat station
sand
toilets
Church Hill

Pony rides on Alnmouth Beach.

71

Alnmouth

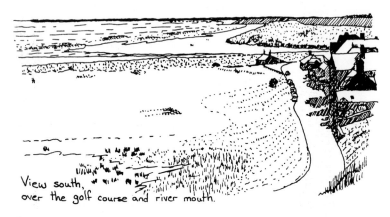

View south,
over the golf course and river mouth.

- <u>Alnmouth</u> is a quiet residential town, with a genteel holiday trade that is catered for by a number of hotels and guest houses. There are sheltered moorings for small craft, a golf course and magnificent beaches. The main street boasts several shops and places to eat. One little window onto the street holds a reminder of the town's former economic importance as a port: a barometric station, courtesy of a Duke of Northumberland.
- At the top of the town there is a <u>Franciscan Friary</u>. The friars have a superb view southwards along the golden coastline to Amble, Hauxley and Coquet Island. Even the "Nine Men of Lynemouth" can be seen on a good day.

Alnmouth seen from Church Hill.

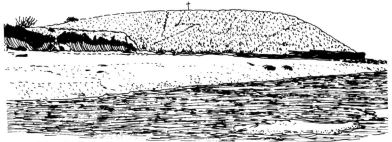

Church Hill

The tall buildings that give Alnmouth much of its character
owe their origins to the granaries of the mediæval port.
This was an important grain port then. But the shipping
has gone, and the town has changed its function. There
are no quays now. Even the river has changed its course.
A great storm in 1806 cut a new channel to the sea,
separating Church Hill from the rest of the town. The storm
also wrecked the Norman church on the hill. A new church
was built in the town, and the ruins on Church Hill
crumbled away. Only a few foundations of the even more
ancient Saxon church of St. Waleric remain. The harbour
silted up, dunes covered the old river mouth, and the
harbour buildings disappeared (except for a ruinous chapel).

The present town is quite well served by public transport, with
frequent buses to Alnwick, and south to Warkworth and
Newcastle. Occasional buses operate to Boulmer.

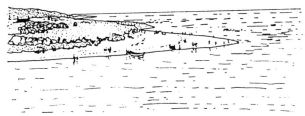

The Aln winds down from
Lesbury, seen from the
Alnmouth - Boulmer road.

• Lesbury Church. dates
from Norman times. The
tower and chancel are
13th century.

Lesbury:
quiet suburbia;
hedges, gardens and
magnificent trees.

74

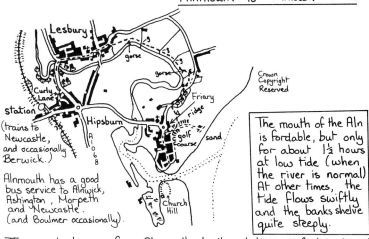

The mouth of the Aln is fordable, but only for about 1½ hours at low tide (when the river is normal) At other times, the tide flows swiftly and the banks shelve quite steeply.

* The quickest way from Alnmouth to the station, on foot, is straight up the main road. But if you have time, go along by the river.
If you have not already climbed up onto the ridge beside the Friary, do so, and enjoy the view south. Take the path beside the Friary, close to the trig. point and descend steeply by the edge of the wood. (If you have already been up the hill you can cheat by walking up the lane from the roundabout at the top of Alnmouth). As you follow the lane past the wood the hedge on the left drops away. Follow a descending path down and across the fields by the river.
As you approach Lesbury the path disappears near a gorse patch. Rise up across the field, and carefully locate the way out of the field: a narrow way between a bungalow and its garage, with a sign-post at the road-end.
Follow the road through Lesbury. The east end is pleasantly suburban, much influenced by the presence of RAF Boulmer, with its massive radar installations. Pass the church and continue through the older part of the village, with its golden sand-stone and beautiful trees.
At the main road, turn down to the old bridge, still carrying the main A1068 road. Cross carefully. On the south side, the wall beside the road is all that remains of a farm-house. Beyond, the footpath is segregated from the narrow road, behind a hedge of magnificent trees. At a road junction, bear right up the aptly-named Curly Lane, that delivers you to the head of the station approach.

75

The rescue helicopter from RAF Boulmer is a frequent sight as it makes sorties up and down the coastline. Give the crew a friendly wave: it may make their day!

North of Birling Carrs, looking north towards Alnmouth.

The approach to Warkworth from the north is magnificent. The road from the beach brings you down to the north end of the mediæval bridge, with its unusual defensive Tower. Cross over the Coquet, into the town.

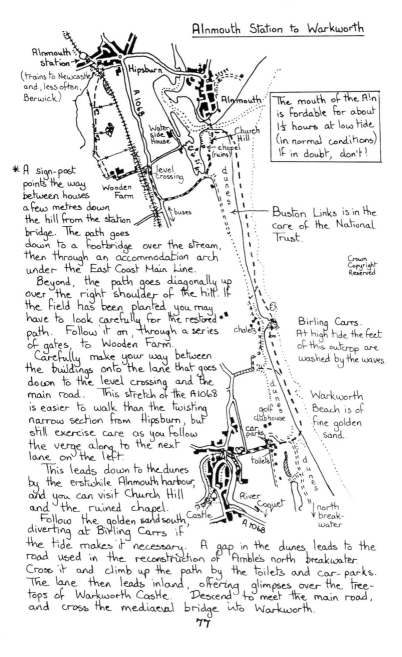

Alnmouth station → (trains to Newcastle and, less often, Berwick)

Hipsburn

A 1068

Alnmouth

Water side House

Church Hill

chapel (ruins)

level Crossing

Wooden Farm

buses

d u n e s

The mouth of the Aln is fordable for about 1½ hours at low tide (in normal conditions) If in doubt, don't!

Buston Links is in the care of the National Trust.

Crown Copyright Reserved

Birling Carrs. At high tide the feet of this outcrop are washed by the waves.

chalets

Warkworth Beach is of fine golden sand.

d u n e s

golf clubhouse

car parks

toilets

d u n e s

River Coquet

north break-water

Castle

A 1068

* A sign-post points the way between houses a few metres down the hill from the station bridge. The path goes down to a footbridge over the stream, then through an accommodation arch under the East Coast Main Line.

Beyond, the path goes diagonally up over the right shoulder of the hill. If the field has been planted you may have to look carefully for the restored path. Follow it on, through a series of gates, to Wooden Farm.

Carefully make your way between the buildings onto the lane that goes down to the level crossing and the main road. This stretch of the A1068 is easier to walk than the twisting narrow section from Hipsburn, but still exercise care as you follow the verge along to the next lane on the left.

This leads down to the dunes by the erstwhile Alnmouth harbour, and you can visit Church Hill and the ruined chapel.

Follow the golden sand south, diverting at Birling Carrs if the tide makes it necessary. A gap in the dunes leads to the road used in the reconstruction of Amble's north breakwater. Cross it and climb up the path by the toilets and car-parks. The lane then leads inland, offering glimpses over the tree-tops of Warkworth Castle. Descend to meet the main road, and cross the mediaeval bridge into Warkworth.

77

Warkworth

— must not be rushed nor passed by. Here is one of Northumberland's treasures. The town sits in a loop of the River Coquet, with a castle at the top of the street. The river provides superb protection on three sides, and the castle on the hill protects the southern approach. Pause awhile in Warkworth, and enjoy its offerings:

● **The bridge**, at the north end, dates from Norman times. It has a defensive tower, through which all traffic had to pass until recently (when the new bridge was built alongside). Few towns in England have anything like this. (The wooden doors of the tower sport a fascinating collection of nails, used to pin up the public notices of centuries!)

● **Church of St. Lawrence**, standing by the river at the foot of the main street. This largely Norman church is built on Saxon remains, and is worth a visit. Respect it as a place of worship, not just as an antiquity. Not all visitors have shown respect— in 1174 the Scots massacred the men, women and children of the town, who had gathered in the church for refuge.

● **The riverside path** runs right round the town — becoming a lane on the eastern side. From the bridge, it runs west past St. Lawrence, and on round the bend of the river. It is a charming walk at any season. Here is the Coquet at its best, cloaked in beautiful trees. You should make time to follow the path upriver — come back to do it if necessary. You will reach a boat landing beneath the castle walls, where you may be able to hire a rowing boat. Walk on up the path (or row up the river) for more romantic scenery: the castle looks down on this stretch through a frame of magnificent trees.

● **The Hermitage** lies upstream about a half-mile beyond the castle. It is on the north bank, and only accessible across the ferry from the riverside path. Here, carved into the rock, is a cell comprising chapel, confessional and dormitory. Various legends surround its purpose, but its real history is still obscure.

● **The town** is an unspoiled Northumberland village. The street runs down from the castle towards the church, then veers off to the bridge. There are a few shops, public houses and a post office. Buses run north to Alnmouth and Alnwick, south to Amble, Ashington and Newcastle.
  Behind the frontages the gardens maintain the mediaeval property pattern, running in long narrow strips towards the river. Those on the east side are bisected by the direct footpath between castle and bridge — another fascinating digression.

A winter evening in Warkworth:
a view upstream from the bridge.
Below: the Norman bridge itself,
with a backcloth of spring trees.

Warkworth

Warkworth Castle dominates, over the river and the town:

Warkworth Castle

- The Castle has been here, in some form since at least 1139. Then Henry, son of the King of Scotland, was made Earl of Northumberland. Later it became the property of the Percy family it was greatly strengthened. It was a bastion against the Scots, and a symbol of national power too. This is the castle of Harry Hotspur, featuring in Shakespeare's Henry IV (part 1).

The castle declined during the Percy family's absence from Northumberland, after their fall from favour, but they gave it their attention again in the 18th century, before finally choosing Alnwick as their family seat.

Now 'English Heritage' maintain it and open it to the public.

The gatehouse.

Warkworth to Amble.

Warkworth Castle from the east

Amble: the yacht-moorings and marina development site

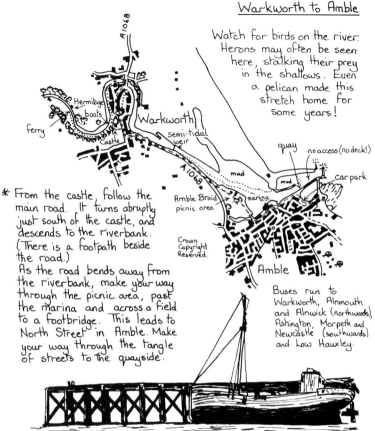

Watch for birds on the river.
Herons may often be seen
here, stalking their prey
in the shallows. Even
a pelican made this
stretch home for
some years!

* From the castle, follow the
main road. It turns abruptly
just south of the castle, and
descends to the riverbank.
(There is a footpath beside
the road.)
As the road bends away from
the riverbank, make your way
through the picnic area, past
the marina and across a field
to a footbridge. This leads to
North Street in Amble. Make
your way through the tangle
of streets to the quayside.

Buses run to
Warkworth, Alnmouth
and Alnwick (northwards),
Ashington, Morpeth and
Newcastle (southwards)
and Low Hauxley.

• <u>Amble</u> is a solidly-built, business-like town. It used to rely on
the export of coal from its own pit (and others) that was
brought down to the staithes by rail. You may notice the
gaps in the town where the tracks came through, and the
staithe, now without tracks or trucks.
   Some grain is still shipped out, and some fish are still
landed. But mainly Amble survives as a resort. There
are golf links, a developing marina, fishing (from the pier
and by boat) and marvelous sands stretching down the coast.
It also caters for the residential, refreshment and entertainment
needs of its visitors.

83

Amble

The south pier terminates with a red and white navigation beacon.

Fishing vessels such as the MV 'Sunshine' can still be seen alongside the quay.

The white house on Pan Point is now a private residence. It was the coast-guard station for many years.

- <u>Coquet Island</u> is famous as the abode of Cuthbert, the Northumbrian saint, who occupied the Benedictine Cell on the island as a hermit, until persuaded to accept the bishopric by the abbess of Whitby, Elfreda, when she visited the isle in AD 684. Other hermits have lived here too: St. Henry of Coquet was a Dane who dwelt here in the 11th century. The Scots captured it in 1645 despite a large garrison of 200 men.

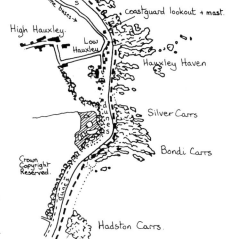

dunes

quay

no access to pier (no deck)

car park

Pan Point

Warkworth Harbour

picnic area

marina

Coquet Island.

monks cell

car parks

buses to Widdrington, Ashington, Morpeth.

AMBLE - BY - THE - SEA

dunes

some buses →

sandy beach (heavily populated on fine summer days)

coastguard lookout + mast.

High Hauxley.

Low Hauxley

Hauxley Haven

dunes

Silver Carrs

Crown Copyright Reserved.

Bondi Carrs

dunes

Hadston Carrs.

* From the quayside in Amble follow the edge of the pool round to Pan Point. Cross this inland of the erstwhile coastguard station (now a private residence). Descend to the rocky beach if possible, and follow it south round Hauxley Point. Alternatively, pick a route along the dunes or even along the quiet road to Low Hauxley, and the footpath beyond.

Druridge Bay

View south towards Cresswell and Lynemouth.

Looking north along the dunes, towards Hauxley and Coquet Island.

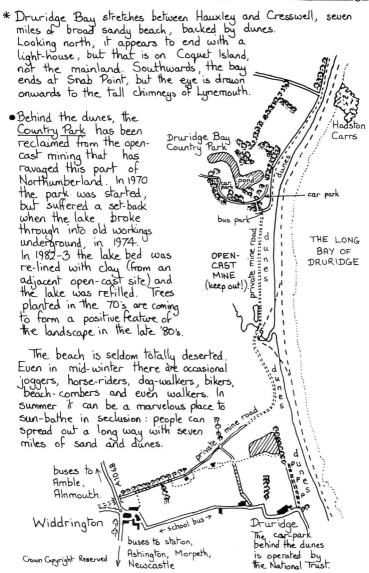

* Druridge Bay stretches between Hauxley and Cresswell, seven miles of broad sandy beach, backed by dunes. Looking north, it appears to end with a light-house, but that is on Coquet Island, not the mainland. Southwards, the bay ends at Snab Point, but the eye is drawn onwards to the tall chimneys of Lynemouth.

• Behind the dunes, the <u>Country Park</u> has been reclaimed from the open-cast mining that has ravaged this part of Northumberland. In 1970 the park was started, but suffered a set-back when the lake broke through into old workings underground, in 1974. In 1982-3 the lake bed was re-lined with clay (from an adjacent open-cast site) and the lake was refilled. Trees planted in the 70's are coming to form a positive feature of the landscape in the late '80's.

The beach is seldom totally deserted. Even in mid-winter there are occasional joggers, horse-riders, dog-walkers, bikers, beach-combers and even walkers. In summer it can be a marvelous place to sun-bathe in seclusion: people can spread out a long way with seven miles of sand and dunes.

Hadston Carrs

Druridge Bay Country Park

car park

pond

car park

bus park

OPEN-CAST MINE (keep out!)

private mine road

dunes

THE LONG BAY OF DRURIDGE

dunes

private mine road

dunes

buses to Amble, Alnmouth.

A1068

Widdrington

← school bus →

buses to station, Ashington, Morpeth, Newcastle

Druridge
The car-park behind the dunes is operated by the National Trust.

DUNE PEAPS

87

Druridge to Lynemouth

Winter shadows,
Cresswell Beach.

Horses are an important part of
the local scene. On roadside
verges and commons across the
district you will see them tethered
to graze. Pie-balds seem to be
much in favour. These are not
the mounts of the rich, or even
of teenage girls, but sturdy
working horses. Their breeding
and maintenance is a long local
tradition. Sometimes they can
be seen pulling little carts – on
land or in the fringes of the sea.
    The latter is in conjunction with sea-coaling, another
activity local to the north-east. Sea-coal is washed
ashore all along the coast. Some is not much larger
than dust, and is gathered with a shovel. But some is
in decent-sized lumps. Much of this comes from the coal
seams that rise in the sea-bed. It burns well – providing
what you have is coal rather than black stone! – and there
is a thriving local trade, with coalers licensed by the Coal
Board.

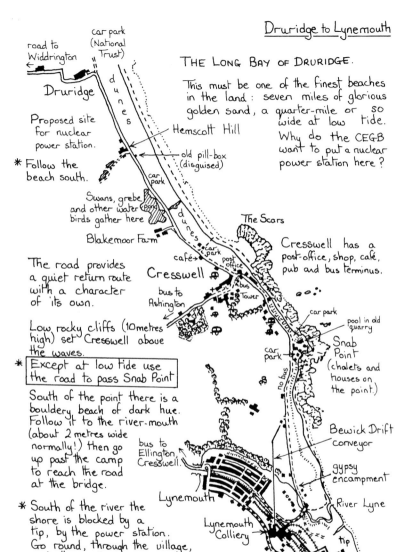

road to Widdrington ←

car park (National Trust)

Druridge

dunes

THE LONG BAY OF DRURIDGE.

This must be one of the finest beaches in the land : seven miles of glorious golden sand, a quarter-mile or so wide at low tide.

Proposed site for nuclear power station.

Hemscott Hill

Why do the CEGB want to put a nuclear power station here?

* Follow the beach south.

old pill-box (disguised)

car park

Swans, grebe and other water birds gather here

dunes

The Scars

Blakemoor Farm

café

car park

post office

Cresswell

bus tower

Cresswell has a post-office, shop, café, pub and bus terminus.

bus to Ashington

The road provides a quiet return route with a character of its own.

car park

car park

pool in old quarry

Low rocky cliffs (10 metres high) set Cresswell above the waves.

no bus

Snab Point (chalets and houses on the point.)

* Except at low tide use the road to pass Snab Point

South of the point there is a bouldery beach of dark hue. Follow it to the river-mouth (about 2 metres wide normally!) then go up past the camp to reach the road at the bridge.

bus to Ellington Cresswell.

Bewick Drift conveyor

gypsy encampment

River Lyne

Lynemouth

* South of the river the shore is blocked by a tip, by the power station. Go round, through the village, past the colliery.

Lynemouth Colliery

tip

The Bewick Drift conveyor continues its slope down, out under the sea, where the dangerous work of mining coal continues.

bus to Ashington

Alcan power station

Crown Copyright Reserved

Lynemouth to Newbiggin Point

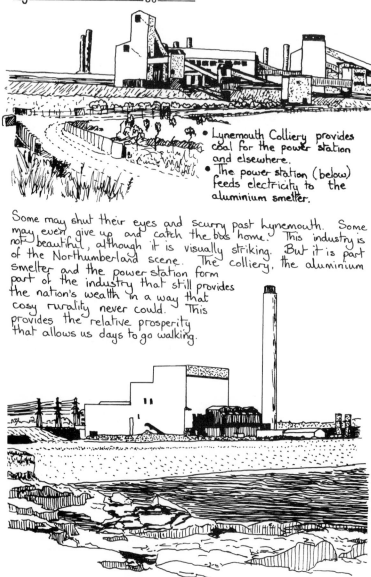

- Lynemouth Colliery provides coal for the power station and elsewhere.
- The power station (below) feeds electricity to the aluminium smelter.

Some may shut their eyes and scurry past Lynemouth. Some may even give up and catch the bus home. This industry is not beautiful, although it is visually striking. But it is part of the Northumberland scene. The colliery, the aluminium smelter and the power station form part of the industry that still provides the nation's wealth in a way that cosy rurality never could. This provides the relative prosperity that allows us days to go walking.

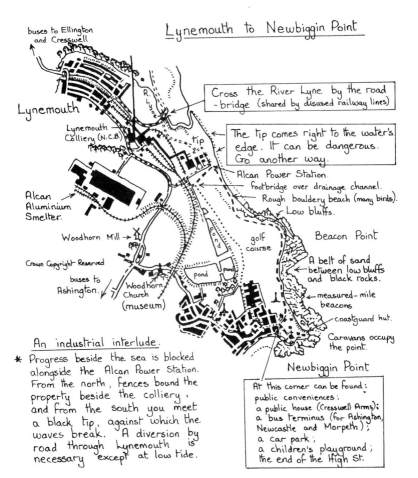

Lynemouth to Newbiggin Point

buses to Ellington and Cresswell

R. Lyne

Lynemouth

Lynemouth Colliery (N.C.B.)

tip

Alcan Aluminium Smelter.

Woodhorn Mill

Crown Copyright Reserved

buses to Ashington.

Woodhorn Church (museum)

golf course

pond

pond

pond

Beacon Point

Newbiggin Point

Cross the River Lyne by the road-bridge (shared by disused railway lines)

The tip comes right to the water's edge. It can be dangerous. Go another way.

Alcan Power Station.
Footbridge over drainage channel.
Rough bouldery beach (many birds).
Low bluffs.

A belt of sand between low bluffs and black rocks.

measured-mile beacons

coastguard hut.

Caravans occupy the point.

At this corner can be found:
public conveniences;
a public house (Cresswell Arms);
a bus terminus (for Ashington, Newcastle and Morpeth);
a car park;
a children's playground;
the end of the High St.

An industrial interlude.

* Progress beside the sea is blocked alongside the Alcan Power Station. From the north, fences bound the property beside the colliery, and from the south you meet a black tip, against which the waves break. A diversion by road through Lynemouth is necessary except at low tide.

* The path along the seaward side of the golf-course is not a public right of way. It is much better than the right of way, which leads from a housing estate across the edge of the dunes, beside tall fencing and taller embankments, to a railway bridge beside the power station. For a return route, the road past Woodhorn Mill and Church is better.

Newbiggin Point enjoys an attractive church, and suffers a sprawling caravan park. The church, and the headland promenade, are worth a visit.

Newbiggin

- St. Bartholomew's, the "church on the point", dates back to the early 13th century. Its spire has been a landmark for North Sea mariners since the 14th century.

  From the headland the view south is extensive on a clear day. You can see Blyth, with its great silos and long jetty. Beyond, the slender white column of St. Mary's Island lighthouse can be seen, followed by the tall grey ruins of Tynemouth Priory. The pink and white lighthouse is on Lizard Point, beyond Marsden Bay.

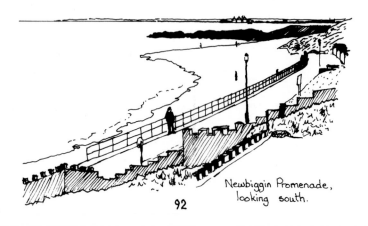

Newbiggin Promenade, looking south.

Newbiggin

- <u>Newbiggin-by-the-Sea</u> is a small seaside town, out of fashion as a resort, and now losing its sandy beach. Once the sands were much higher, almost up to the level of the present promenade. Now this itself has had to be protected from the ravages of the sea by heaped boulders. Even so, the sea has wrecked some of the gardens above the promenade.

The golden sand is speckled with the black of sea-coal, that comes from the seams that outcrop into the sea just north and south of the town. One of the characteristic sights of the area is the sea-coaler, toiling up from the sea with four or five bags of coal perched on a bicycle.

Newbiggin was a thriving port in mediaeval times, and still is home to a number of the distinctive cobles, with their deep prows and shallow sterns. Tractors are driven into the surf in all weathers to launch or retrieve the cobles — and also the lifeboat.

Newbiggin Point to the River Wansbeck.

* Follow the promenade round the bay, past the life-boat station, the slipway and 'The Ship'. At the south end of the bay you can rise up to the level of the town, and find a footpath that dips into the valley of a little stream. Alternatively, you can explore the rocks at the end of the bay, locating the Needle's Eye (a hole through the rocks that you may have spotted from the promenade). From the rocks you can make your way up the little valley to join the path.

You climb up southwards past modern residences that guard their privacy with high wire fences and guard-dogs. But their location reminds me of King Canute.

The wire-lined channel leads you to the cliff-edge, and a marvelous view down the coast past the mouth of the Wansbeck. Cambois power stations dominate the sky-line, but closer at hand are the black strata that under-lie Newbiggin. There is coal in there. But they are at the foot of the cliffs. The tops are loose and crumbly, so don't go too near the edge!

As you pass the ranks of caravans of the holiday centre, you will find that the cliff-edge path has been eroded so that you are forced to divert into the caravan park.

Descend onto the sandy spit that juts out towards Cambois, but DO NOT TRY TO CROSS THE RIVER HERE.

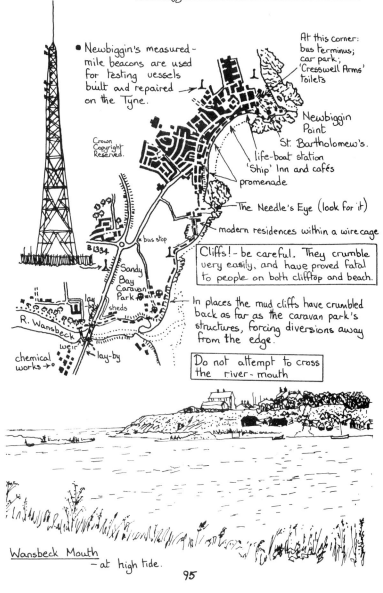

- Newbiggin's measured-mile beacons are used for testing vessels built and repaired on the Tyne.

Crown Copyright Reserved.

At this corner: bus terminus; car park; 'Cresswell Arms' toilets

Newbiggin Point
St. Bartholomew's.
life-boat station
'Ship' Inn and cafés
promenade

The Needle's Eye (look for it)

modern residences within a wire cage

Cliffs! - be careful. They crumble very easily, and have proved fatal to people on both clifftop and beach.

× bus stop

B 1334

Sandy Bay Caravan Park

In places the mud cliffs have crumbled back as far as the caravan park's structures, forcing diversions away from the edge.

lay-by
sheds

R. Wansbeck

weir   ← lay-by

chemical works →

Do not attempt to cross the river-mouth

Wansbeck Mouth
— at high tide.

95

Wansbeck Mouth

• The <u>Wansbeck weir</u> and <u>lock</u> form an essential part of the Wansbeck Riverside Park. Before it was built, the river from Sheepwash down had undistinguished boggy banks that were washed and hung up to dry untidily by every tide. Now there are good paths all the way from the river-mouth to Sheep -wash, through well-designed and wooded parkland near Ashington. If you want a major digression, or just a change from beaches, follow the river's north bank upstream past Ashington to Sheepwash. You could even continue across the fields to Bothal, with its castle and Saxon church, both nestling in a wooded elbow of the Wansbeck Valley. Beyond, paths through Bothal Woods would lead you to Morpeth. (and from Sheepwash, Bothal or Morpeth you could even catch a bus back to Newbiggin or Sandy Bay!)

The mouth of the Wansbeck is a quiet and peaceful place. The points almost meet, leaving a narrow channel to allow the Wansbeck to greet the sea, and enclosing a haven for small boats. On the north side there are solidly-built lock-ups to cater for the sailors and fishermen, whilst on the south side cluster solid but weather-beaten huts, reminiscent of photos of Victorian and Edwardian England. Here men come to relax: work on their boats, fish or enjoy quiet conversation or contemplation. It is difficult to remember, that the world of international industry begins just a few hundred metres away (unless the wind happens to be blowing from the direction of the chemicals plant!)

At low tide many of the boats sit on the sand or mud, and a way can be found along the shore on the south side, avoiding the crumbling cliff. But at high tide the water laps right up to the low muddy cliff, making progress difficult: go round!

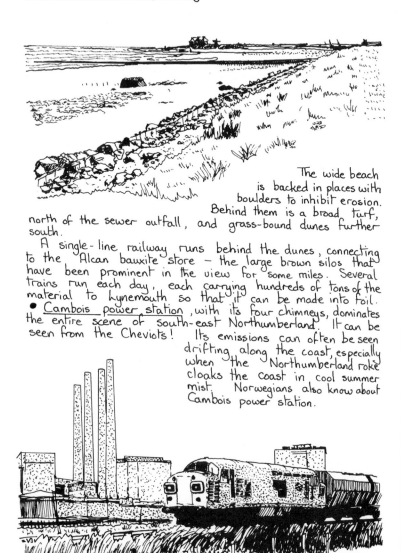

The wide beach is backed in places with boulders to inhibit erosion. Behind them is a broad turf, north of the sewer outfall, and grass-bound dunes further south.

A single-line railway runs behind the dunes, connecting to the Alcan bauxite store — the large brown silos that have been prominent in the view for some miles. Several trains run each day, each carrying hundreds of tons of the material to Lynemouth so that it can be made into foil.

• Cambois power station, with its four chimneys, dominates the entire scene of south-east Northumberland. It can be seen from the Cheviots! Its emissions can often be seen drifting along the coast, especially when the Northumberland roke cloaks the coast in cool summer mist. Norwegians also know about Cambois power station.

* From the weir a track passes under the main road, and turns to run alongside it for ½ km, to join the Glaxo access road. Turn left, joining the road next to the level crossing. Follow it eastwards.

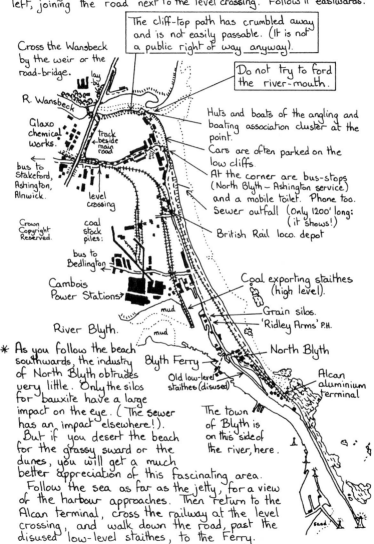

The cliff-top path has crumbled away and is not easily passable. (It is not a public right of way anyway).

Do not try to ford the river-mouth.

Cross the Wansbeck by the weir or the road-bridge.

lay-by

R. Wansbeck

Glaxo chemical works.

track beside main road

bus to Stakeford, Ashington, Alnwick.

level crossing

Crown Copyright Reserved.

coal stock piles.

bus to Bedlington

Cambois Power Stations

mud

River Blyth.

mud

Huts and boats of the angling and boating association cluster at the point.

Cars are often parked on the low cliffs.

At the corner are bus-stops (North Blyth – Ashington service) and a mobile toilet. Phone too.

Sewer outfall (Only 1200' long: it shows!)

British Rail loco. depot

Coal exporting staithes (high level).

Grain silos.

'Ridley Arms' P.H.

North Blyth

Blyth Ferry

Old low-level staithes (disused)

Alcan aluminium terminal

The town of Blyth is on this side of the river, here.

Sand.

* As you follow the beach southwards, the industry of North Blyth obtrudes very little. Only the silos for bauxite have a large impact on the eye. (The sewer has an impact elsewhere!).

But if you desert the beach for the grassy sward or the dunes, you will get a much better appreciation of this fascinating area.

Follow the sea as far as the jetty, for a view of the harbour approaches. Then return to the Alcan terminal, cross the railway at the level crossing, and walk down the road, past the disused low-level staithes, to the Ferry.

Blyth Harbour

- Blyth Harbour is a key part in the economy of south-east Northumberland. It developed with iron, but Bedlington Ironworks closed more than a hundred years ago. Then the coal trade developed enormously, and this continues. The high-level staithes at Cambois (below right) discharge efficiently into colliers, the coal coming by rail from the pits around Ashington and further north, and also from the open-cast mines. The inefficient low-level staithes have outlived their usefulness, and have lost their rails (below).

  You may be fortunate enough to watch a large ship enter the harbour, such as the Lord Hinton (above) coming to load coal, and dwarfing the buildings of the town.

  Ship-building, a long tradition on the river, has gone. But now there is a bauxite terminal (middle, right), where vast quantities are unloaded from ship, stored in the huge silos, and despatched by rail to Lynemouth. A roll-on, roll-off freight terminal for trade with Scandinavia has been developed. Blyth adapts to meet the trade of the times.

  It is also home to the Royal Northumberland Yacht Club!

The long
curved jetty protects
the mouth of the Blyth,
and can be seen to advantage from a hillock beyond
<u>the bauxite terminal</u> (below)

Blyth : Ferry to South Beach

* From the 'Ferryman' follow the boundary wall of Wimborne Quay round the corner to the main road. Going towards the centre of town you pass some public toilets, the 'Travellers' Rest Hotel', and the 'Porthole'. Turn left with the main road, bypassing the town centre. A narrow alleyway, just beyond the Marine Engineering yard, offers a way down onto the quay.

  Just opposite is the Alcan bauxite terminal, with its great silos and grab hoist. You may be fortunate enough to watch a ship unloading, with hoses playing to lay the dust.

  Follow the quay south, past the central concrete section and the wooden staithes. The lifeboat and the Pilot boat berth at the south end. Leave the quay and pass the gate of South Harbour, and walk up to <u>Ridley Park</u>.

You enter the park past a flower-bed made from a redundant boat, and a triple war-memorial. The park is a delight of lawns and trees, bowling greens and play-areas for kids. There are pavilions for the various clubs, and public toilets. Nor is it locked in by railings. It is a park for people, a place to savour and enjoy.

The park is named after Viscount Ridley, who gave this park to the town. (He was Home Secretary from 1895 to 1900).

* At the South end of the park join the main road. You pass the Ridley Park Hotel, then enter a viewless ½ kilometre: suburban houses on the right, a tall fence bordering a timber yard to the left. Opposite the Wellesley Nautical School you may be able to escape into the South Harbour, to the pier and the beach. Otherwise continue — another ½ km of fence — to two large houses, that mark the start of South Beach. You have a choice here: beach or promenade.

102

Blyth: Ferry to South Beach

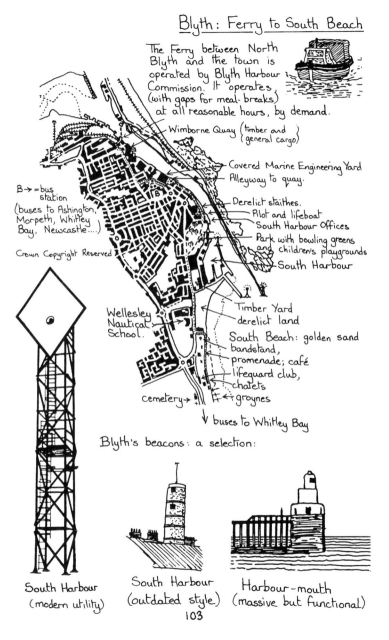

The Ferry between North Blyth and the town is operated by Blyth Harbour Commission. It operates, (with gaps for meal-breaks) at all reasonable hours, by demand.

Wimborne Quay (timber and general cargo)

Covered Marine Engineering Yard
Alleyway to quay.

Derelict staithes.
Pilot and lifeboat
South Harbour Offices
Park with bowling greens and children's playgrounds
South Harbour

B → = bus station
(buses to Ashington, Morpeth, Whitley Bay, Newcastle....)

Crown Copyright Reserved

Wellesley Nautical School.

Timber Yard
derelict land

South Beach: golden sand
bandstand,
promenade; café
lifeguard club,
chalets
groynes

cemetery →

↓ buses to Whitley Bay

Blyth's beacons: a selection:

South Harbour
(modern utility)

South Harbour
(outdated style)

Harbour-mouth
(massive but functional)

103

Blyth South Beach to Seaton Sluice

Blyth Beach : golden sand, held in place by huge groynes.

● Seaton Sluice – the harbour.
   The sluice gates once dammed the river upstream of the
present bridge. At low tide, when the harbour bed was
exposed, it could be ploughed up using teams of horses.
Then the gates were opened and the rush of water took
away the silt, maintaining a deep harbour.

Blyth South Beach to Seaton Sluice

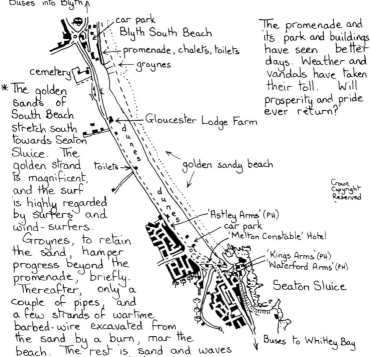

Buses into Blyth

car park
Blyth South Beach

promenade, chalets, toilets

groynes

cemetery

Gloucester Lodge Farm

d u n e s

toilets

golden sandy beach

d u n e s

'Astley Arms' (PH)
car park
'Melton Constable' Hotel

'Kings Arms' (PH)
'Waterford Arms' (PH)

Seaton Sluice

Buses to Whitley Bay

The promenade and
its park and buildings
have seen better
days. Weather and
vandals have taken
their toll. Will
prosperity and pride
ever return?

* The golden
sands of
South Beach
stretch south
towards Seaton
Sluice. The
golden strand
is magnificent,
and the surf
is highly regarded
by surfers and
wind-surfers.

Groynes, to retain
the sand, hamper
progress beyond the
promenade, briefly.
Thereafter, only a
couple of pipes, and
a few strands of wartime
barbed-wire excavated from
the sand by a burn, mar the
beach. The rest is sand and waves
and sea-birds — and the view.

Approaching Seaton Sluice.

<u>Seaton Sluice</u> : an industrial past.

● Seaton Sluice is a charming little pleasure-port, with a few small boats riding the Seaton Burn. Grassy banks and houses, plus a collection of public houses present an almost rural picture. Yet for hundreds of years this was an important place of industry, until about 1870.

Hartley Pans was the old name. From the 13th century, when local coal-mining began, the mouth of the burn was the location of huge, coal-fired salt pans, where sea-water was evaporated. This trade flourished until 1782, when the government imposed heavy salt taxes. The legal trade dwindled (and salt-smuggling occurred) until new regulations killed it completely in 1798.

Coal was also shipped from here. By 1660 the harbour was inadequate, and a pier was built to protect the mouth of the harbour. The ingenious sluice followed in 1690, to avoid silting problems. The Delaval family initiated the works (with some government finance). By 1761 more work was necessary, and the cut was blasted through the headland to provide a second harbour entrance.

The extraction of copperas from the pyrites in the local coal measures was also carried on in the town. A major industry, between 1763 and 1871, was the glass-works and bottle-factory. Brick-making, brewing and quarrying were other local industries.

The Gut, now blocked.

The north
harbour-entrance.
(The skyline features
chimneys at Cambois and
Lynemouth, the Blyth silos
and cranes, and St. Bartholomew's
at Newbiggin).

Seaton Delaval Hall.

- Seaton Delaval Hall lies a mile up the hill from the round-about. It is not normally open to the public, but is a grand sight even from the road. Despite extensive fire damage (in 1752 and 1888) it remains a superb example of Vanbrugh's work. It was built (1718-29) for Admiral George Delaval. The family were associated with the area from Norman times, and were responsible for much of the harbour and industrial development of the area. They also had a reputation for gaiety and practical joking, around 1800 — houseguests might find themselves tipped from bed into cold baths, for example!

Seaton Sluice to St. Mary's Island.

The sea-wall round Collywell Bay.
The large stack in the bay is Charlie's Garden. One Charlie Dockwray had an allotment on the top. Despite the exposed site, it reputedly produced the earliest cabbages and potatoes in the village!

Between Seaton Sluice and Curry's Point (opposite St Mary's Island) sandstone cliffs face the pounding seas. These are the scene of many shipwrecks. On 28th October 1880 a ship ran onto the rocks. Thomas Langley, of Hartley, volunteered to be lowered down the cliff-face by rope. He rescued four people. On his way home he heard that another ship had run aground. He seized a line and battled his way through the surf to the ship. All the crew were saved.

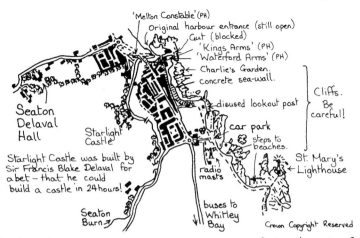

'Melton Constable' (PH)
Original harbour entrance (still open)
Cut (blocked)
'Kings Arms' (PH)
'Waterford Arms' (PH)
Charlie's Garden.
concrete sea-wall.
disused lookout post
Cliffs.
Be careful!
car park
steps to beaches.
St. Mary's Lighthouse
Seaton Delaval Hall
Starlight Castle
Starlight Castle was built by Sir Francis Blake Delaval for a bet — that he could build a castle in 24 hours!
radio masts
Seaton Burn
buses to Whitley Bay

Crown Copyright Reserved

* From the road-bridge over the burn you can follow the side of the harbour round to the cut, and venture across the bridge to the peninsula if you wish. But the way south is to follow the old road above the sea-wall. You pass two ways down to the foot of the cliff, and then, next to a seat, a gateway opens onto a footpath along the cliff-top.

Follow the path, crossing the beach access road, and cut the corner inland of the derelict lookout post. You pass a caravan site, a car park, and an impressive array of radio masts. The path continues along the cliff-top. Please note the warning signs — the cliff edges are loose and crumbly. Watch your feet whilst moving; <u>stop</u> to admire the view!

Whitley Bay

Footbridge over Brierdene Burn.

• The pleasure-domes of Whitley Bay: the "Spanish City" contains a permanent fair-ground, with roundabouts, roller-coasters and all sorts of rides, plus games of skill and chance, together with the usual showbiz noise and glitter.

The town of Whitley Bay is built on top of a sandstone cliff, that is now almost invisible under the stone and concrete of the promenades. In winter they are almost deserted, but continue to protect the town. In summer the cafes open, and people throng them.

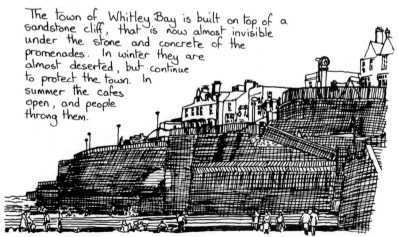

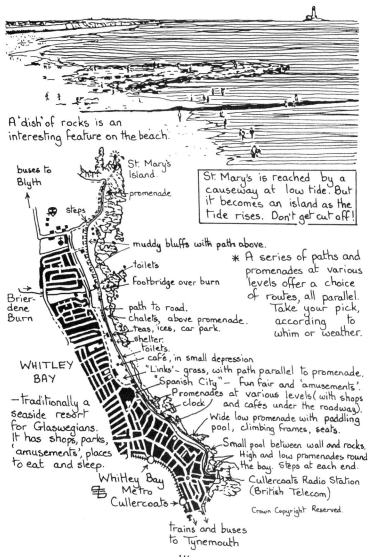

A 'dish' of rocks is an interesting feature on the beach.

St. Mary's Island.

promenade

buses to Blyth

steps

St. Mary's is reached by a causeway at low tide. But it becomes an island as the tide rises. Don't get cut off!

muddy bluffs with path above.

toilets

footbridge over burn

Brier-dene Burn

path to road.

chalets, above promenade.

teas, ices, car park.

shelter.

toilets.

café, in small depression

WHITLEY BAY

"Links"- grass, with path parallel to promenade.

"Spanish City" - fun fair and 'amusements'.

- traditionally a seaside resort for Glaswegians. It has shops, parks, 'amusements', places to eat and sleep.

Promenades at various levels (with shops and cafés under the roadway).

clock

Wide low promenade with paddling pool, climbing frames, seats.

Small pool between wall and rocks. High and low promenades round the bay. Steps at each end.

* A series of paths and promenades at various levels offer a choice of routes, all parallel. Take your pick, according to whim or weather.

Cullercoats Radio Station (British Telecom)

Whitley Bay Metro

Cullercoats →

trains and buses to Tynemouth

111

Cullercoats

<u>View over the Lifeboat Station.</u>

* Cross Cullercoats Point on the footpath by the Radio Station. This installation, now operated by British Telecom, was one of the earliest marine radio stations when opened in 1908. Go down onto the promenade, and walk along towards the harbour. You pass an electricity board sub-station, in an elegant circular building with a viewing platform on top. It is rather better than the usual offerings! Climb up again to a higher promenade. Above the Lifeboat Station, decide whether to go down the ramp and cross the harbour floor, or walk round the promenade above the cliff.

<u>Cullercoats</u> from the south side of the harbour.

Cullercoats.

● The two large buildings on the beach are the <u>Lifeboat House</u> and the <u>Dove Marine Laboratory</u>. The latter is run by Newcastle University and has an aquarium open to the public.

The harbour is a natural haven, protected by the headlands and the rocky underwater spurs, assisted by the two breakwaters.

* On the south side of the harbour, pass the breakwater and the lifeguard's hut onto the headland. Hidden from the main road you will find the <u>Smugglers' Cave</u>, a large natural arch and cave. But <u>Cullercoats</u> is better known as an old fishing port than for smuggling, although the Cullercoats fish-wives no longer carry creels of fish for sale throughout Northumberland.

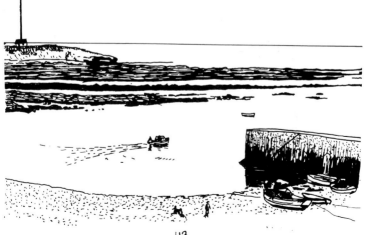

Cullercoats to Tynemouth Priory.

Sharpness Point.

* From the point south of Cullercoats Harbour, follow the beach or the promenade south. You pass St. George's, with its 180' spire. The church is Victorian, reflecting much of Tynemouth housing. The beach is sandy, with cafés, swings and sun-bathers in summer. Above there are green lawns and flowery gardens. The Plaza's grandeur is now host just to amusements and fish and chips. Opposite, the gardens enclose an open-air boating pool. Behind it, the Tyneside Metro runs, the little electric trains providing a fast and efficient service.

An open-air swimming pool nestles below the cliffs as you approach Sharpness Point. Turning the corner, you meet Tynemouth Bay, with its sand, cliffs, steps — and the view of the point, with Priory, Castle and coastguard station.

Cullercoats to Tynemouth Priory.

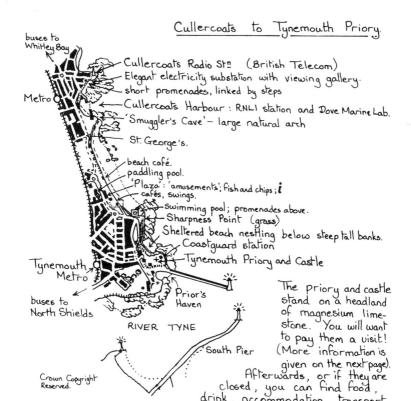

buses to Whitley Bay

Metro

- Cullercoats Radio Stⁿ. (British Telecom)
- Elegant electricity substation with viewing gallery.
- short promenades, linked by steps
- Cullercoats Harbour: RNLI station and Dove Marine Lab.
- 'Smuggler's Cave' — large natural arch
- St. George's.
- beach café.
- paddling pool.
- 'Plaza': 'amusements'; fish and chips; *i*
- cafés, swings.
- swimming pool; promenades above.
- Sharpness Point (grass)
- Sheltered beach nestling below steep tall banks.
- Coastguard station
- Tynemouth Priory and Castle

Tynemouth Metro

buses to North Shields

Prior's Haven

RIVER TYNE

South Pier

Crown Copyright Reserved.

The priory and castle stand on a headland of magnesium limestone. You will want to pay them a visit! (More information is given on the next page).
    Afterwards, or if they are closed, you can find food, drink, accommodation, transport and so on in the town, just up Front St.

Tynemouth

115

Tynemouth Castle and Priory.

The headland at Tynemouth is a natural defensive site, walled on three sides by steep cliffs and the sea. It is also important strategically, dominating the mouth of Northumbria's great east-west artery, the River Tyne.

The church recognised the value of the site at an early date, with a religious house here from about 650 AD until Henry VIII dissolved the Priory in 1539.

Fortifications soon developed too. The Priory defended itself from Danish raids, and then from a succession of armies during the Anglo-Scottish wars. It was formally fortified from 1296 (Licence to crenelate). The costs of defence reduced the once-rich Priory to penury.

Henry VIII knew a good thing when he saw it, and took the castle into royal hands when he dissolved the Priory. In Elizabeth's reign the landward slopes were laid out in contemporary style, with artillery positions and anti-siege earthworks. (as at Berwick) It remained a royal castle, and held a garrison until recently. Modern guns were emplaced during the World Wars, and their sites can still be seen, overlooking the North Pier.

● The modern <u>coastguard station</u> was built on the site of the old barracks. Occasionally the Air-Sea Rescue helicopters land here to transfer casualties to ambulances.

116

Tynemouth Priory.

The coastguard station and Priory, from the west.

- The <u>Castle</u> and <u>Priory</u> are in the care of English Heritage, and can be visited during reasonable daylight hours. Entry is along the access road, close under the walls to the Barbican. Inside the curtain wall you find the ruins of the Priory church. Part of the west end, with a fine doorway, and the towering east front, are the prominent features. Beyond the latter, the 15th century Percy Chapel still has its roof, with fine vaulting with carved bosses. The monastic buildings used to lie on the south side of the church, but little remains. To the south-east is a large graveyard. Amongst the gravestones is one for Corporal Rollo, who held the lantern for the burial of Sir John Moore at Corunna.

Do visit the eastern ramparts, for the view of the mouth of the mighty Tyne.

The Castle Barbican.

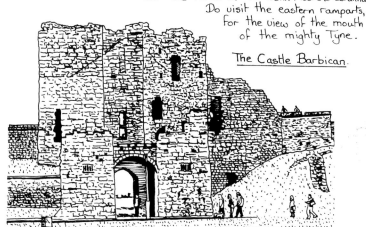

117

Tynemouth to North Shields Fish Quay.

Collingwood Monument.

* From the end of Front Street, opposite the Castle Barbican, follow the road that descends towards the river. At the foot of the bank turn left and head for the North Pier. Pass the travelling crane and walk out to the platform by the lighthouse (provided that conditions are favourable, of course!) From here you have an excellent view: the headland itself; the river-mouth; and the coast stretching away northwards past St. Mary's lighthouse, and south along the rising cliffs to the candy-striped light on Lizard Point, Marsden.

The piers were built to enable ships to leave the rivermouth in unfavourable conditions. Started in 1854, they had poor foundations and were badly damaged by storms. They were completed in 1890, breached two years later and then rebuilt.

* Return to the shore. The haven on your left, used by a sailing club, is Prior's Haven. Cross the line of the erstwhile railway (that used to connect with the North Eastern Railway up in the town).

Now you have a choice of routes. You can follow the road onto the promontory and then descend to the riverside path past the Life Brigade Watch House, or you can follow a footpath to the right, past the monument.

The Life Brigade was established to save life here, after a series of horrific wrecks on the Black Middens. These lurk just below the surface at high tide, on the north side of the river. Also overlooking the scene is the statue of Admiral Lord Collingwood, born in Newcastle and Nelson's second-in-command at Trafalgar.

A variety of footpaths now leads you on towards North Shields, on or above the riverside promenade. Look for:

* the High and Low Lights – white light-houses marking the passage.
* the South Shields Groyne, tipped with a squat red lighthouse. This was built to prevent the river-mouth silting up.
* the Life-boat station (too small for the present boat)
* the Pilot boat (and moorings at South Shields).
* Clifford's Fort, built to defend the river from the Dutch in 1672. It now houses kipper curing-houses, and the Low Light.
* The Fish Quay, home for the North-Shields fishing fleet.

The "Esso Severn", a coastal tanker, enters the River Tyne past the Fish Quay. Tyne Street, up by the High Light, is a superb vantage point for watching the river.

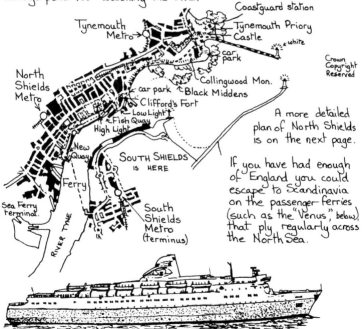

Coastguard station

Tynemouth Metro →

Tynemouth Priory Castle

← white

car park

Collingwood Mon.

Black Middens

car park

North Shields Metro ↓

Clifford's Fort

Low Light

Fish Quay

High Light

New Quay

SOUTH SHIELDS IS HERE

Ferry

Sea Ferry terminal.

RIVER TYNE

South Shields Metro (terminus)

A more detailed plan of North Shields is on the next page.

If you have had enough of England you could escape to Scandinavia on the passenger ferries (such as the "Venus", below) that ply regularly across the North Sea.

119

North Shields

- The High and Low Lights at North Shields are leading lights. When lined up they indicate the deep-water passage for ships entering or leaving the Tyne. The sand-banks shift over the years, so there has been a succession of lights since 1540. The present High Light (up on Tyne Street) and Low Light (down next to the Fish Quay) are dated 1808 on their stonework. A plaque recalls their rebuilding in 1860. Operation is automatic.

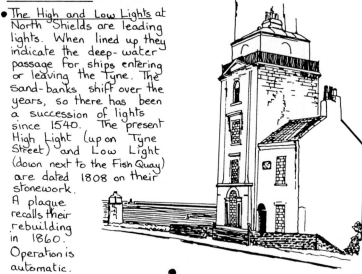

- The Old High Light was built in 1727 by Trinity House. Note that the seaward side is painted black to avoid confusion with the present High Light.

The steep banks below the Lights were once crammed with houses clustering around the many flights of steps that still link the two levels. Conditions were appalling, with only rudimentary water and sewage services. The banks were cleared in the 1930s, and are now covered in grass, bushes and trees.

The area between Tyne Street and the main town has also been covered in slums in the past. The most recent (built 1956) have now been pulled down, and new houses are being built.

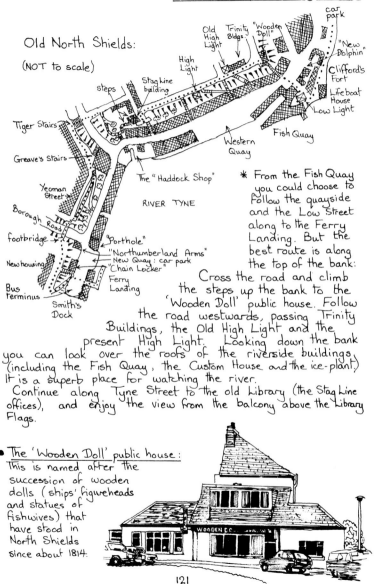

Old North Shields:

(NOT to scale)

car park

"New Dolphin"

Clifford's Fort

Lifeboat House

Low Light

Fish Quay

"Wooden Doll"

Trinity Bldgs

Old High Light

High Light

Stag line building

steps

Tiger Stairs

Greave's Stairs

Yeoman Street

Borough Road

footbridge

New housing

Bus Terminus

Smith's Dock

The "Haddock Shop"

RIVER TYNE

Western Quay

"Porthole"

"Northumberland Arms"

New Quay : car park

"Chain Locker"

Ferry Landing

* From the Fish Quay you could choose to follow the quayside and the Low Street along to the Ferry Landing. But the best route is along the top of the bank:

Cross the road and climb the steps up the bank to the 'Wooden Doll' public house. Follow the road westwards, passing Trinity Buildings, the Old High Light and the present High Light. Looking down the bank you can look over the roofs of the riverside buildings, (including the Fish Quay, the Custom House and the ice-plant.) It is a superb place for watching the river.

Continue along Tyne Street to the old Library (the Stag Line offices), and enjoy the view from the balcony above the Library Flags.

• The 'Wooden Doll' public house: This is named after the succession of wooden dolls (ships' figureheads and statues of fishwives) that have stood in North Shields since about 1814.

WOODEN DO...

121

• The Literary and Philosophical Society of Tynemouth built the library in 1806-7. The building was taken over in 1895 by the Stag Line Shipping Company, who used it until 1980. The Stag emblem still embellishes the south exterior wall.

Just by the library a balcony overlooks the river at the head of a flight of stairs — the Library Flags. These were rebuilt after a landslip: read the inscription above the steps.

• Down below, the 'Haddock Shop' is now deserted. This used to be a specialist repair yard for light-vessels.

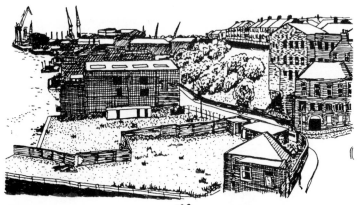

* From the north side of the Library (away from the river) a stairway leads down Ranter's Bank. It twists and turns, past buildings that have disappeared, down to a garden just above Liddell Street. A footpath leads across, and then up Magnesia Bank. Follow it through the gardens and up to Union Street. Turn left, descending briefly to a junction with Bedford Street, then go straight ahead up Tiger Stairs. Turn left again, past new housing and the top of Greave's Stairs, and past Oliver's Engineering works. Either walk along Yeoman Street or along the terrace just below, to the footbridge over Borough Road (This, incidentally, was a toll road, cut by the Railway to speed access to the station).

Beyond the bridge, continue past more new housing to a vantage point overlooking Smith's Dock. This ship repair yard is now the heart of Tyneside ship repair work, and a fascinating collection of vessels can usually be seen.

A ramp leads down to the bus terminus, the New Quay, and the South Shields Ferry.

The Library
(Stag Line office),
from Liddell St.

Shields Ferry

If you have enjoyed the coastline of Northumberland, you will probably also enjoy its continuation southwards along the edge of the old County Durham : South Shields, Frenchman's Bay, Marsden Rock and Roker Sands await your delectation.

The Shields Ferry is the first stage in a new adventure... or the last stage in this one : cross the Tyne by ferry to see this river from the proper angle — there is plenty of public transport in South Shields to take you home!

Bibliography.

These books have proved informative and entertaining, and as such are suggested for further reading. They are arranged in no particular order, of merit nor anything else.

'Lindisfarne'   Magnus Magnusson,   Oriel (R+K.P.) 1984
'Northumberland' Nikolaus Pevsner + Richmond, Penguin 1957
'Portrait of Northumberland' Nancy Ridley, Robert Hale 1965
'Northumbrian Heritage' Nancy Ridley, Robert Hale 1968
'The Northumberland Coast' Keith Proud, Discovery Guides 1984
'Northumbria' Harold Wade, Geographia
'The Long Bay of Druridge' Henry Tegner, Frank Graham 1968
'Northumbria in Colour' H.S. Thorne, Thorne's Univ? Bk 1966
'A History of Embleton Parish Church' Oswin Craster, Embleton P.C.
'Northumberland Memories' Robin Gard, Frank Graham 1981
'Northumberland Yesteryear' Robin Gard, Frank Graham 1978
'North Shields Riverside Trail' Tyne and Wear County Council.
'A Story of Amble' Wilkinson + Morrison, Amble Council.
'Songs and Ballads of Northern England' T+G Allan (Newcastle)
'Hartley and Old Seaton Sluice', Thomas Earnshaw 1961
'Looking around Northumberland' Harry Rowland 1979
'The Natural History of Dunstanburgh Castle Point'
                    Sir John Craster, HMSO 1963
'Discovering Northumberland' T.H. Rowland, Frank Graham 1973
'Walks for Motorists — Northumberland', R.A., Fred? Warne 1981
'The Wildlife of Northumbria' William Balmain, Frank Graham 1971
'North Northumberland for the Walker', H.O.Wade + W. Balmain,
                    Northumberland Gazette.
'Ramblers through Northumberland' Ramblers Assoc?, FrankGraham,77
'The Reivers Way', H.O.Wade, Frank Graham 1977
'Newbiggin-by-the-Sea in old picture postcards', Will? Harrison,
                    European Library in Zaltbommel.
'Walks on the Northumberland Coast', N. County Council 1983
'Walker's Britain' Ordnance Survey + Pan Books 1982
'Walker's Britain 2' Ordnance Survey + Pan Books 1986
'Birdwatcher's Britain' Paslow, O.S + Pan Books 1983
'The National Trust Guide to the Coast', Tony Soper,
                    Webb + Bower (Exeter) 1984
'Comprehensive Guide to Northumberland' Tomlinson,
                    David + Charles, reprint 1968
'Northumberland — a Shell Guide' Thomas Sharp, Faber 1937/69
'Ordnance Survey Leisure Guide; Northumbria', OS/AA 1987
'Northumbria in Pictures' Beryl Scott Sandhill 1986

Index

Symbols used on the Sketch Maps.

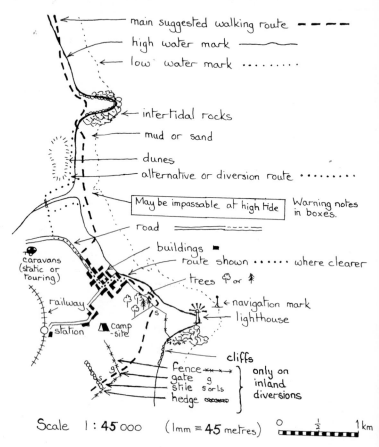

main suggested walking route — — — —

high water mark ——————

low water mark ·········

← intertidal rocks

mud or sand

dunes

alternative or diversion route ········

May be impassable at high tide | Warning notes in boxes.

road

buildings ■

route shown ······ where clearer

trees ♀ or ♠

caravans (static or touring)

← navigation mark

lighthouse

railway

station

Camp-site

cliffs

fence ×—×—×
gate g
stile s or l.s
hedge

} only on inland diversions

Scale 1 : 45 000   (1mm ≡ 45 metres)   0 —— ½ —— 1 km

The routes shown are not necessarily rights of way. There are some permissive paths, and some rights of way. For specific information use the Ordnance Survey maps.

Remember too that things change. The coast-line is very active. Erosion can change cliffs, alter coastal streams, destroy paths. New paths may be agreed, or others closed.